Below: *Harwich harbour in the eighteen-nineties, with the guardship* HMS Mersey *at her moorings. In the Pound are the steam lifeboat* City of Glasgow, *on station at Harwich between 1894 and 1901, and R. & W. Paul's tug* Spray.

ivic pomp
ant-at-
rman
uty
ney,
er a

HARWICH
gateway to the continent

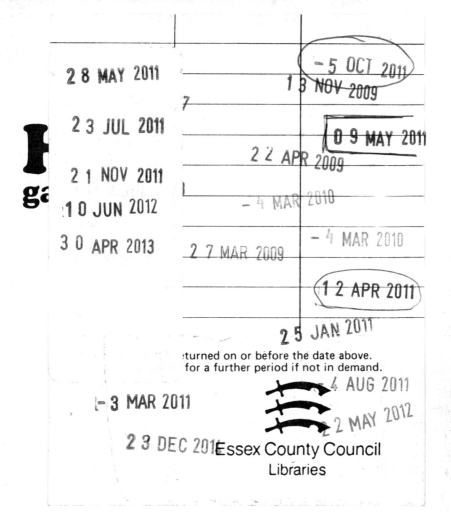

TERENCE DALTON LIMITED
LAVENHAM . SUFFOLK
1990

Published by

TERENCE DALTON LIMITED

ISBN 0 86138 048 7

Text photoset in 10/11pt Times

Printed in Great Britain at
The Lavenham Press Limited, Lavenham, Suffolk

Contents

Chapter one	'A Pretty Town'	1
Chapter two	The Harwich Packets	5
Chapter three	'A Town of Hurry and Business'	9
Chapter four	Harwich for the Continent	19
Chapter five	The Spreading Town	37
Chapter six	Pro Bono Publico...	53
Chapter seven	Educating the Young	65
Chapter eight	Sons of the Sea	73
Chapter nine	Life Ashore	91
Chapter ten	The Changing Scene	103
Acknowledgements	... ...	118
Index	... ...	119

'A Pretty Town'   1

"ON WEDNESDAY last, I went to Harwich, which I had not seen this 27 years. My Lord, it is a place to make much of, for the haven hath not its fellow in all respects not in this realm." These words were written to Lord Burghley by Lord Howard of Effingham in 1588 when he put into Harwich after defeating the Armada, and they are no less true today.

The town stands at the tip of a peninsula in north-east Essex commanding the entrance to a magnificent harbour, where the Orwell flows down from Ipswich to meet the waters of the Stour. Since Alfred destroyed a Viking fleet of sixteen ships there in 885 AD, Harwich and the harbour have played a vital part in our national story.

By a charter of 1604 the borough incorporated the old seaport and the village of Dovercourt, which lay to the west and is now the residential suburb. While *Druvrecurt* is recorded in the Doomsday survey of 1087, Harwich is not mentioned before 1196, when it was called *Herdwic*, *Herewyche* or *Herewiz*. Shortly before that date the town had been planned and laid out on a typical medieval plan by Roger Bigod, Earl of Norfolk, who was Lord of the Manor of Dovercourt. His thinking is clearer when we recall that the Stour has changed its course. It had originally entered the sea to the north of Felixstowe, where the Romans had built Walton fort to guard the entrance, but in the course of time that entrance silted up and the river burst through the marshy land to take its present course. The

Earl realized that a fortified town on the promontory which lay a few miles to the north of Dovercourt could give him control of the harbour, and prove a source of profit from tolls, harbour dues, admiralty rights, rents and the "profits of justice".

Throughout history Harwich has played an important role as a naval base in times of war. When Edward III began the Hundred Years' War he left Harwich with over two hundred ships to destroy the French fleet off Sluys at the mouth of the Scheldt. That was in 1340.

Despite opposition from Ipswich, a royal licence was obtained in 1352 to collect tolls from ships entering the harbour in order to build a wall on the seaward side of Harwich; the defences were further strengthened in the sixteenth century by Henry VIII and his daughter Mary.

In August, 1561, Queen Elizabeth came to Harwich, which she described as "a pretty town". During her visit she met some of the men who took an outstanding part in the struggle with Spain, among them Thomas Gray, commander of the *Ark Royal* at the defeat of the Armada in 1588, Roger Hankin, master of Raleigh's flagship at an attack on Cadiz in 1599, and his brother John, who commanded Drake's flagship the *Revenge*. Christopher Newport commanded an expedition to the West Indies, sacked four Spanish towns, and joined other ships in the Azores to await three richly laden carracks. For four days they lay in wait, then on 3rd August, 1592, Captain Thomas Thompson of Harwich sighted the *Madre do Dios*, a three-decker of 1,600 tons, drawing 31 feet of water; her capture was no small thing, for her cargo was valued at £150,000.

Newport is more famous in Virginia than in his native town, for he led the expedition which founded the colony at Jamestown in 1607, thirteen years before Christopher Jones and his ship the *Mayflower* sailed with the Pilgrim Fathers. The descendants of John Alden, a Harwich man who was related to Jones and sailed with him to New England, are proud to belong to the Society of the Alden Kindred of America.

By 1600 the cod fishery was well established, and Harwich ships were also engaged in bringing "sea coals" from the Tyne to London, but trade was greatly hampered by the attacks of French privateers called Dunkirkers. After the Civil War the Commonwealth showed determination to protect our shipping from such dangers and to challenge the maritime

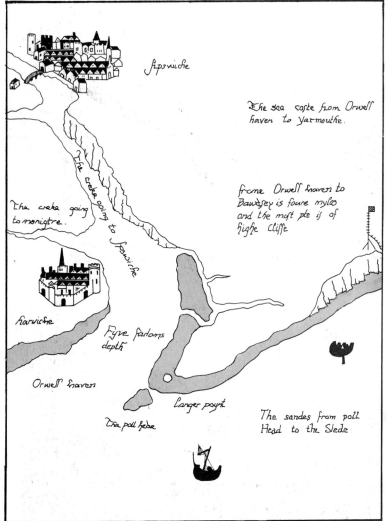

Left: *The town of Harwich and Orwell Haven as it was during the reign of King Henry VIII. Harwich was surrounded by a town wall, and in 1539 the King's commissioners found that the townspeople in an unusual display of enthusiasm had dug two trenches and built two earthwork batteries to defend town and harbour. "Ye should have seen the women and children work with the shovels at the bulwarks there," wrote the Earl of Oxford with obvious approbation.*

Opposite page: *The treadwheel crane from the Naval Yard, built in 1667 at a time when King Charles II was reforming the Royal Navy and warships were being built at Harwich. It was re-erected on Harwich Green in 1930.*

supremacy of the Dutch. War with the Dutch resulted, and Harwich was the obvious place to establish a naval station where ships could be victualled and repaired. After the restoration of Charles II in 1660 a golden age began for the Royal Dockyard, where some of the finest ships were designed and built by Sir Anthony Deane, the master shipwright. The first was the *Rupert*, a third rate of 66 guns, followed by the *Resolution*; after Deane had moved to Portsmouth his foreman, Isaac Betts, continued building warships to his designs.

In 1672 it was decided to close the Harwich yard as a permanent base and to transfer it to Sheerness, but when a Dutchman became King William III of England in 1689 and began a period of hostility towards France, Harwich again became a centre of maritime activity. Three warships were built in 1694, and hulks were sunk to form breakwaters on the east and west sides of the yard. When peace came in 1713 the yard passed into private hands.

Mail Packet "Princess Royal", leaving Harwich. c. 1810.

The Harwich Packets 2

FROM time immemorial Harwich ships have taken passengers to the Continent. In 1434 three were licensed to carry pilgrims to the shrine of St James at Compostella in Spain, and mention is made of vessels carrying mail and passengers to Holland early in the seventeenth century, but the first recorded regular service began in 1661, when the Postmaster General and the City of Amsterdam agreed that all mail between England and the United Provinces should be sent through Harwich in English ships. The vessels were of the type known as hoys and were called packets because their prime function was to carry packets of mail, but they also carried freight and passengers at a single fare of twelve shillings first class and six shillings second class.

Up to 1676 the terminus on the Dutch side was Helvoetsluis, but when George Fox, William Penn and other leading Quakers took the packet boat in 1677 they landed at Brill, where their vessel was forced to lie at anchor all night. The English sailors disliked the dangerous shallows outside Brill, and for most of the eighteenth century the packets used Helvoetsluis. Heavily armed against enemy privateers, they were always ready to chase prizes themselves if the opportunity arose.

Things changed after 1689 when William of Orange ascended the throne of England. He was in Harwich on four occasions and stayed in Church Street at the house of Captain Thomas Langley, who called himself "Commander of the Packet Service" and for £80 a month ran a twice-weekly service to the Continent. This arrangement came to an end when William announced in 1694 that the Surveyor to the Navy Board would provide four fast, low-built boats which would normally sail unarmed; the dangerous and time-wasting practice of chasing prizes was to end. Captains were instructed to "run while you can, fight when you cannot run, and throw the mails overboard when fighting will no longer avail". Such a policy was not popular with the men, but from the point of view of the passengers and the Post Office it proved very successful.

After 1714, when the Elector of Hanover became King George I, members of the royal family, ministers, ambassadors and the families of the minor German princes often passed through Harwich, where they were suitably received by the mayor. The diary of the artist Sir John Thornhill, who crossed to Holland in 1711, gives a valuable illustrated description of the borough and the boats. There were five boats: the *Dolphin*, commanded by Captain Maddison Hunt, who was then mayor of Harwich; the *Eagle*, Captain Stevenson; the *Marlborough*, Captain Cole; the *Prince*, Captain Lucas; and the *Dispatch*, Captain Phillipson. There were also five "passage boats" which sailed between Harwich and London on Tuesdays and Saturdays at a single fare of three shillings to connect with the continental service. Travellers by road took the coach from the Saracen's Head, Aldgate, and stayed the night at Witham; the coach fare was sixteen shillings.

Sir John Thornhill's party, consisting of

three gentlemen and their servants, paid £2 2s 6d for a passport which was surrendered to the commissioner's clerk, Mr Bickerton. He issued them with single tickets costing twelve shillings and sixpence for each gentleman and six shillings and sixpence for each servant, and received a tip of five shillings. The boats hoped to sail at about 2 pm on Thursdays and Sundays, but adverse weather could delay their arrival or departure by a week or more. Then, as W. H. Lindsey observed in *A Season at Harwich*,

> the town became one vast lodging house, from the numerous passengers waiting to be conveyed; for though the inns were spacious enough for all ordinary occasions, they could not find sleeping room for parties thus detained, with, probably, many friends and relatives who came to bid them adieu.

The external appearance of the boats changed little before 1800. The *Eagle*, a typical

One of the "pacquett boates" can be seen, marked L, on J. Kip's engraving of Harwich about 1713. The town was still surrounded on two sides by a rampart, though this would have proved scant defence if an attack had been made.

packet, built at Arundel in 1703, was a round-sterned sloop, 53 feet long and 18½ feet beam, with "a large Cabin or State Room, good windlas, suit of masts and yards, caps and cross trees". She was about 60 tons and carried a hundred passengers, in addition to a crew of twenty.

The journal of Sophie la Roche, who made the crossing in 1786, gives a picture of the scene below deck:

> Two rooms and two cabins hold 26 berths for passengers; it is all very attractive. The outer room is panelled with mahogany, and has a fine mirror and lamp brackets fastened to the wall. The berths are arranged along the side walls like theatre boxes, one above the other; they have thoroughly good mattresses, white quilted covers, neat curtains, and, on a ledge in the corner, is the chamber, made of English china, used in case of sickness. In order to lie down, the outer board of these boxes is removed and then fitted in again by the sailors, to prevent people from tumbling out. It holds one person quite comfortably, and the whole looks very neat.

Sophie was at sea for forty-eight hours and like most of the passengers was violently sick. John Wesley, then eighty-three years old, was also on that boat and after twenty-four hours of bad weather comforted everybody with a sermon

based on the text: "It is appointed unto men once to die."

The crossing was always uncomfortable. At times conditions could be very bad, as Matthew Todd, a "gentleman's gentleman", found when he set out from Harwich in 1814 to accompany his master on the Grand Tour. The seventy-five passengers were forced to go below, where there were bunks for twelve; the rest lay on the floor. Those in the bunks were thrown out so that everyone lay "bread and butter fashion" in layers, "and no chance of getting out, as the door of the cabin had about half a dozen people sleeping against it".

Bad weather was not the only cause of delay; captains and crews, deprived of the privilege of prize money, were quick to seek other perquisites. The inlets of the Essex and Suffolk coast were a paradise for smugglers, and the fast packet boats with their shallow draught were apt to disappear mysteriously for days at a time, even when the wind was in the most favourable quarter. In Sir John Thornhill's time a captain's pay was £10 a month; a master received £3 10s, a boatswain £2 10s, a gunner £2 10s, a carpenter £3 5s, and a surgeon £3 10s; but much more could be made from smuggling, overcharging for food and accommodation on board, bribery, and swindling the Post Office, so that a captain was said to make a good £1,000 a year in peacetime, and £1,500 in wartime. Griffith Davies, Collector of Customs at Harwich, wrote in 1764 that:

> one of the Captains of the Pacquets income annually, was more than that of all the officers of the Customs in the whole port, put together.

Captain Cockerill, a packet captain for about twenty years, raised a large family and left £30,000, a fabulous fortune in those days and worth around £1 million at today's values.

During the War of American Independence (1776–83) two of the packet boats were captured. The *Prince of Orange* was taken in May, 1777, by a large lugsail vessel mounting eight six-pounders and twelve swivel guns and flying the rebel ensign of thirteen red and white stripes, but the enemy ship was captured by the

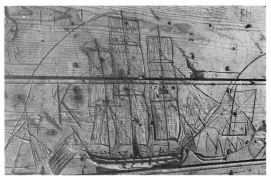

French, who had not yet entered the war, and the packet was returned to her master, Philip Deane. Among the pictures cut by prisoners on a wall of the former gaol in the Guildhall in Church Street is one of a ship flying the American flag, under the date 1777.

The service from Harwich was interrupted when Holland was occupied by the French during the Revolutionary and Napoleonic Wars, both the Harwich packets and those from Dover being transferred to Yarmouth, whence they sailed to Gothenburg in Sweden. When peace was concluded in 1801 the nine packets resumed sailings from Harwich to Helvoetsluis, but on the resumption of hostilities in 1803 the *King George* was seized at Helvoetsluis; Philip Deane, who had succeeded his father as captain, died after four years in captivity.

When war ended in 1815 the days of the Harwich packets were numbered. They began to suffer from the competition of the Dover–Calais service, which introduced steam paddle-boats of much greater tonnage than the Harwich packets. Though ten of these steamships were actually built in the Navy Yard at Harwich by George Graham, the local masters stuck to sail; as a result, when the Post Office services were put out to tender in 1831, the offer of the General Steam Navigation Company to operate steamers from Tilbury was accepted. The following year the service left Harwich, which unlike Tilbury was not then served by a railway. This was a heavy blow, for it was reckoned that the packet service had provided work for nearly two hundred people.

'A Town of Hurry and Business'   3

IN HIS *A Tour Through the Whole Island of Great Britain*, published in 1724, Daniel Defoe described Harwich as "A town of hurry and business, not much of gaiety and pleasure, yet the inhabitants seem warm in their nests, and some of them are very rich". This view of the town was confirmed by Parson Woodforde, who wrote in his diary in 1777: "Have been in Harwich, that is in a hurry all the day long. It took its rise from King George the First landing at Harwich for the first time of his coming to England."

The packet boat captains enjoyed great influence in civic affairs at a time when bribery and corruption were rife in both local and national politics. The charter of 1604 had nominated the first mayor, councillors and aldermen, and until 1835 vacancies were filled by co-option. Among the thirty-two members of the council were the captains and the agent of the packet boats, most of whom were related. They were appointed by the Postmaster General on the recommendation of the council, and their prime duty was to further the interests of their employer when the council elected two MPs to represent the borough. Other members were employed as customs officers and obeyed the orders of the Treasury. All had a personal interest in returning the Government nominees to Westminster, and a succession of men connected with the Treasury represented Harwich until the Reform Act of 1832.

The prosperity of the eighteenth century changed the appearance of Harwich; many new houses were built and old ones were given new frontages. Government tax figures show that the number of houses in Harwich rose from 233 in 1670 to 375 in 1766, and to 487 in 1801, indicating that work was available and people were moving in from neighbouring villages to live in a town which fulfilled the function of a market, a port, a centre of maritime activities, and a seaside resort.

Until 1784 the town crier rang his bell at 8 am on Tuesdays and Fridays to open the market; it filled Market Street with stalls, which spilled over into adjacent thoroughfares, until its closure at 8 pm. Farmers at Dovercourt sent food; labourers who grew vegetables and kept a pig also supplied the market. Women came from nearby villages, often by ferry from Suffolk, to sell butter and eggs. Hawkers and hucksters who added to the congestion by setting up their stalls frequently appeared in court for causing obstruction in Currents Lane, King's Quay Street, Eastgate Street and Castlegate Street.

The council decided in 1784 to build a market hall on corporation land on the corner of King's Quay Street and Outerpart East, a site measuring 68 feet by 36 feet. It was enclosed on two sides by a wall which faced the road, and entrance gates led to an open yard in the middle of which was a building where the public scales and weights were kept. Around this building were stalls for garden and dairy produce, poultry and fish; the Shambles, where butchers had their stands, were built against the wall and had a roof over them. A Clerk of

Lord Anson departing from Harwich with the Royal Caroline *and four other royal yachts in 1761. He was to bring Princess Charlotte of Mecklenburg-Strelitz from Holland to wed King George III. In the background is the Naval Yard with HMS* Arrogant, *a 3rd rate of 1,644 tons and 74 guns, nearing completion. On the right are sunken hulks serving as breakwaters.*

the Market was appointed to collect dues, inspect food, detect fraud, and check weights and measures. To judge from the cases at the Quarter Sessions, most tradesmen tried to defraud customers in some way.

Although most men gained a livelihood from maritime activities, many women supplemented the family income by spinning wool into yarn for weaving. This could bring a wife three shillings a week. An advertisement for a new master of the workhouse, which stood on the site of the present St Nicholas's vicarage, asked for a man able to comb wool and supervise the work of old ladies in spinning. Until the end of the century the demand for yarn was brisk, but it slowed down with the increasing use of machinery and the fall in exports due to the French wars. There was never much weaving done in Harwich, and this had died out by 1800.

The list of sailings in and out of Harwich in the *Ipswich Journal* shows a steady increase in the number and size of vessels using the port. Ships came from Scandinavia with timber and iron, but the chief trade was in coal from the Tyne and Wear. The return voyage took a fortnight and all business was conducted by the master, who bought the coal and sold most of it in London. However, local trade was considerable; in 1789 around fifty dealers used to come from Colchester, Maldon, Wivenhoe, Burnham, Sudbury and Manningtree to buy coal from the big colliers and take it away in smaller ships.

The five packet boats to Holland and the five passage boats which provided the connecting service between Harwich and London were said to have employed nearly two hundred men; added to this figure were those employed on the twice-daily ferry service to Ipswich and Manningtree. Many more, however, depended on them for a living. These included watermen, porters, customs officers and many others involved in the provision of food, drink, accommodation and transport for travellers.

The eighteenth century saw a rise in the population of Essex and London, with a resulting increase in the demand for food and fuel. Ships sailing from Harwich to the Thames usually took agricultural produce, and from the middle of the century Thomas Cobbold of Harwich supplied malt for London breweries, but the sale of fish also rose rapidly and a revived fishery became a major source of prosperity in the borough. In 1715 there were only three smacks at the port. The number had risen to sixty-four in 1774, when nearly five hundred men and boys were employed in fishing for cod and haddock off Iceland, the Orkneys and the Dogger Bank. The boats were about 40 feet long and 25 tons burden, decked at each end and with a wet well. The fish were kept alive in the well until the boat returned to Harwich, where they were either killed or transferred to a store boat. Most of the catch was sent by road to Billingsgate market.

The fish were caught on lines between four and five miles long, baited with whelks and mussels on hooks six feet apart. As each smack needed about eight hundredweight of bait a week, a large number of local vessels were engaged in dredging for whelks. Others went

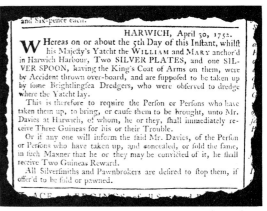

An unfortunate mishap occurred while the royal "Yatcht" William and Mary *was in Harwich harbour in 1752, leading to this advertisement appearing in the* Ipswich Journal.

to Norway and bought lobsters which they sold in London. There were oyster beds in Ramsey Creek and in the marshy channels which lay on the western side of the town, but most of the oysters were taken away to grow and fatten in the estuary of the Colne, while others went to Holland.

Fishing boats often went out at night and brought contraband ashore from larger ships, but smuggling was on a comparatively small scale here, for it was too difficult to move the goods away safely in any large quantity. The inhabitants were sympathetic to the men who supplied them with cheap tea and spirits, and customs men complained that they were "barbarously ill-used". Griffith Davies, who was the Collector of Customs at Harwich for forty years and mayor fifteen times, reported: "We cannot walk in the town without being insulted, and are threatened to be shot or thrown overboard if we go on board the pacquets." After two customs boats had been cut from their moorings and another had had its anchor stolen, he concluded that there was "great reason to believe that malicious persons were responsible". In 1784 the body of John Turner, a customs officer, was found in the harbour. It was reported that "He was seen

A typical cutter-rigged North Sea fishing smack portrayed in a print by E. W. Cooke published in 1829.

late at night walking in the town, and how the accident happened is not known".

The customs cutters *Argus* and *Bee* were stationed at Harwich, and their crews must be commended for their bravery and devotion to duty. They brought many smugglers into Harwich, often after a bloody struggle with desperate men, which sometimes brought tragedy to local families. One of the greatest disasters concerned the *Argus* in September, 1807, when five men of the cutter were killed and eight severely wounded in an action with a French lugger carrying a crew of sixty.

At least once a month the authorities held a sale in Harwich of ships and contraband which had been seized. These usually fetched very low prices, for there was plenty for all. On one occasion 2,100 gallons of gin were sold, together with the equipment and timbers of a brig which had been broken up because it had been specially built for smuggling.

Most of the craftsmen in Georgian Harwich followed trades connected with shipbuilding. Some worked on their own account making sails, blocks, rope, and ironwork, but about a hundred were employed in the shipyard, which after 1713 was in private hands. The Admiralty retained an interest, and when war broke out

with France in 1740 Harwich became a naval station. John Barnard, a shipbuilder of Ipswich, took over the yard and by 1782 had built nineteen warships. The last was the *Irresistible*, a third rate of 74 guns, but before she was completed the men went on strike, saying that there was no money for wages or materials. At that time a labourer could earn seven or eight shillings for a six-day week of twelve hours a day, while a skilled man was paid twelve to fourteen shillings.

Barnard went bankrupt in 1781, and Joseph Graham succeeded him at the yard, where by 1805 he had built nine warships and several merchantmen before he also found himself in financial trouble. He managed to stay in business until he died in 1814, leaving his son George to carry on. The experience of Barnard, Graham and others showed that the shipbuilding industry had peculiar problems, and a full order book was no guarantee of profits. Money could be lost on a contract when the supply of labour and materials was uncertain. Prices fluctuated as timber became scarce, and in times of war shipwrights were impressed to work in Admiralty dockyards. For such reasons ships could not be delivered on time, and penalties were exacted which in

Right: *The twin wheels of the Naval Yard crane revealed when it was dismantled for removal to the Green in 1930. The lack of any effective braking system sometimes led to the load taking control, with consequent injury to those inside the wheels. In 1894, for instance, two men and a lad were using the crane to lift timber; when "the two men stepped out to see if the timber had been hoisted high enough the strength of the lad was not sufficient to prevent the wheels of the crane from running back, and the unfortunate lad was whirled round and round and rendered unconscious".*

Below: *The Naval Yard as it appeared in the middle of the nineteenth century, about the time that the elder Vaux took over the yard from John Bagshaw. The American vessel on the slip, which was taking emigrants from Bremen to New York when it went aground off the Essex coast and was taken into Harwich for repairs, had been hauled out by means of the capstan on the left; as many as sixty men might be employed on this capstan.*

the case of Barnard forced a good man to go to the wall.

From the middle of the eighteenth century attempts were made to develop Harwich as a resort where fashionable people could experience the newly discovered benefits of seawater bathing. In 1753 Mr Hallsted, proprietor of the Three Cups, opened a bath house near Angel Gate; and in the following year Thomas Cobbold set up a rival establishment, known as the Brewer's Baths, on the west side of a lane which later became George Street. Cobbold grew prosperous and soon bought up not only the Three Cups but most of the inns in the borough, including the Trafalgar and Great White Horse at Dovercourt, the Angel, the Swan, the King's Head and the Duke's Head, together with the Castle at Ramsey.

The Assembly Rooms in Castlegate Street were "not remarkable for size or elegance, or often filled with a large and fashionable party" but were a popular rendezvous, especially for dancing, cards and music. The Three Cups was the venue for civic functions and "Assembly balls", and several other inns provided a varied programme of entertainments. In 1753 "the surprising dancing bears" could be seen at the King's Arms.

The Society for the Propagation of Christian Knowledge opened a library in 1710, and by 1800 another library and a billiard room was also made available to the public. A bowling green existed until the War Department put the Ordnance Building on it at the time the Redoubt was built. There was no organized football but cricket was a popular sport among gamblers. In 1750 the *Ipswich Journal* advertised that a Harwich XI would play a Colchester XI for a wager. At such matches a team and its backers put up a stake amounting to £50 or more with the result that there were frequent arguments, stoppages, and unfinished games. The losing team deliberately wasted time; on one occasion only one ball was bowled in the last fifteen minutes before the match ended.

Visitors found much of interest in the Naval Yard. The main entrance was through the great gate adjoining Naval House. Above the

gate the royal coat of arms was carved in stone and brightly coloured, surmounted by a clock, a bell turret and a weather-vane in the shape of a sailor and an anchor. De Rochefoucauld wrote in 1783 that there was no attempt to keep strangers out, and folk wandered freely round the quay, dock, sawpit, steam kiln and boat builders' sheds. He knew of no other dockyard where such a thing would have been allowed.

The importance of the packet boat ferry to Holland meant that the road to London was kept in good repair by turnpike trusts, set up by Parliament between 1695 and 1793 and empowered to raise money by collecting tolls from road users. When Sir John Thornhill came to Harwich in 1711 there were two coaches weekly from London with an overnight stop at Witham, but in 1748 a "flying coach" travelling via Dedham did the journey in a day for nine shillings, and by the turn of the century four coaches each day covered the distance in nine hours.

The presence of soldiers and sailors and their

Above: *A "crane chair" was among the fittings mentioned in an advertisement of 1753 for Mr Hallsted's bath house.*

Opposite page: *"Gentlemen cricket players" at Harwich are mentioned in 1780, and this water colour painted by J. Nixon in 1784 shows a match in progress on Harwich Green.*

Right: *The King's House on the site of the present Trinity House offices was demolished in 1850, soon after this photograph was taken by Mr John Wiggin, of Ipswich. It was built about 1660 by Thomas King.*

This plan of the encampments at Harwich in 1782 shows the line of the quays before the reclamation and development that took place in the eighteen-fifties. There is scarcely a house outside the old town, and the road continues the line of West Street across the Green to what became Harbour Crescent and Barrack Lane. The wells near the road, still visible, were usually let to brewers; most townspeople drank rainwater. The windmill that formerly existed at Harwich has gone, but two are shown at Dovercourt; both were subsequently moved, as can be seen from the 1864 Ordnance Survey map reproduced on pages 48 and 49.

ladies added to the gaiety of the town during the Revolutionary and Napoleonic Wars. Barracks were built on the Beacon Field, and more were put up on what became known as Barrack Field, but the most imposing relic of those years is the great circular Redoubt, constructed in 1807–08, which necessitated the closure of the old London Road and the laying of a new highway on the line of the present Main Road.

In 1801 Nelson came to Harwich in the *Medusa* but disappointed the expectant crowds by remaining on board. The object of his visit was to assist with the organization of a local naval defence force called the Sea Fencibles. In

Harwich they numbered 414, mostly workmen from the Naval Yard, who were reservists and immune from impressment. At the same time a similar force of infantry was raised, known as the Loyal Harwich Volunteers, "to defend His Majesty George III against foreign enemies, or the wicked designs of seditious and disaffected persons" within seven miles of Harwich. The corps elected the mayor, John Hopkins, as its first captain and wore a uniform of "round hats with a sable bearskin, blue pantaloons, a white waistcoat and gaiters". The men were instructed in drill and the use of arms by a sergeant and a corporal from the Cambridge

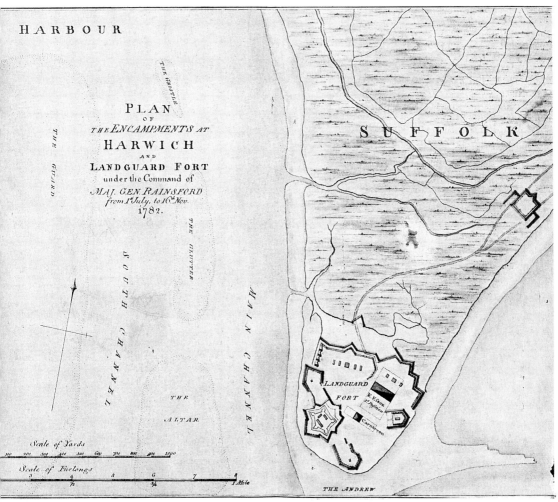

HARBOUR

PLAN
OF
THE ENCAMPMENTS AT
HARWICH
AND
LANDGUARD FORT
under the Command of
MAJ. GEN. RAINSFORD
from 1st July, to 16th Nov.
1782.

THE CENTER

THE GUARD

THE SOUTH CHANNEL

THE CLUTTER

MAIN CHANNEL

SUFFOLK

LANDGUARD FORT

Carnarvon

THE ALTAR

Scale of Yards

Scale of Furlongs

THE ANDREW

Militia. They had a drummer and a fifer, and John Robinson MP presented them with colours. His gift was rejected on the grounds that it was "not only unfit on account of its smallness and inferiority, but is also degrading to the estimation in which so respectable and laudable an Association ought to be held". They accepted instead an offer from Miss Hindes to make a suitable banner for two guineas. A member could resign on payment of five pounds, but the fine was waived in the case of Mr Dukes who asked to resign because he was deaf, and blind in one eye. The committee "considered this reasonable, in view of the fact that he could not hear the word of command".

As the war dragged on poverty became widespread and many people were on the verge of starvation. The Volunteers made secret plans for action in the event of riotous behaviour in their area. The fiftieth anniversary of the coronation of George III in 1809 was celebrated by a meal "for the comfort and enjoyment of full one thousand poor inhabitants". As the total population of the borough was only 2,761 in 1801, this figure must have included nearly every adult. When peace came in 1815 prosperity did not return. For the people of Harwich the prospect was bleak.

Opposite page: *The Corporation Pier, usually known as Halfpenny Pier, was opened in 1853 and the two-storey ticket office seen here was opened the following year. The figure dressed in top hat, frock coat and white trousers is a member of the Harwich constabulary.*
Below: *The ss* Orwell, *which took a party of railway travellers to Rotterdam in 1846.*

Harwich for the Continent   4

HARWICH suffered a heavy blow in 1832 when the Post Office transferred the packet boat service to Tilbury, which had a railway to London. W. H. Lindsey wrote in his *A Season at Harwich* in 1851:

> Fearful have been the struggles that the inhabitants have since been called upon to make; for, while nearly every port in the kingdom has felt the advantages that locomotive steam conveyances confer, Harwich, with its harbour scarcely equalled by any in the kingdom, has been suffered to languish.

The Eastern Counties Railway was formed to build a main line from London to Norwich, and as early as 1836 its engineer John Braithwaite carried out a survey for a branch line to Harwich, but nothing came of it. When the railway reached Colchester in 1843 the company found itself unable to continue. Ipswich businessmen took a leading part in promoting the Eastern Union Railway, which completed the line from Colchester to Ipswich in 1846. Ipswich showed its potential importance as a port for continental traffic when the line was opened in June of that year: a party left Shoreditch Station at half past five in the morning by train for Ipswich where a steamer was waiting to take them to Rotterdam. They reached their destination by ten o'clock that night.

A railway needed a private Act of Parliament to authorize its construction, and in 1844 both the Eastern Counties Railway and the Eastern Union Railway put forward plans for a Harwich branch; both were rejected on the grounds that the expected traffic would not warrant the provision of a railway. There was opposition from Ipswich, and the same thing happened in 1846 when revised schemes were submitted by Braithwaite for the ECR and Joseph Locke, engineer of the EUR. The borough council petitioned Prime Minister Sir Robert Peel to refer the competing plans to the Railway Commissioners as a matter of urgency, pointing out that it was over ten years since the railway was first projected. At last, on 22nd July, 1847, the EUR secured the passage of an Act empowering it to build a line along the south bank of the Stour from Manningtree to Harwich. However, its troubles were not yet over, and financial difficulties, combined with opposition from the ECR, delayed construc-

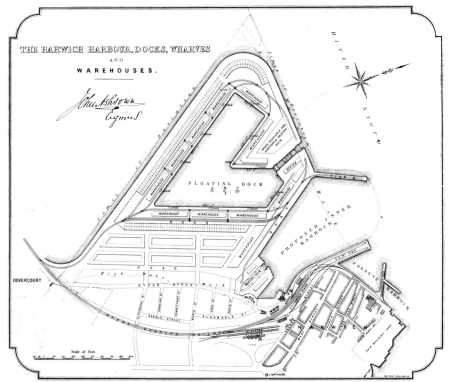

THE HARWICH HARBOUR, DOCKS, WHARVES
AND
WAREHOUSES.

John Ashdown
Engineer

FLOATING DOCK

Plans for docks and warehousing on Bathside were first made in 1846. These proposals date from the eighteen-seventies.

tion until 1853. The ECR entered into an agreement to lease the line upon completion, but in January, 1854, they took over the EUR and were thus responsible for opening the Harwich branch.

Meanwhile preparations were made to provide the necessary facilities for steamship services to operate from Harwich. Schemes were put forward to reclaim the bay, a mile wide, which lay between Harwich and Ray Island. In 1845 it was proposed to enclose the whole area and make a tidal basin within it with a quay on the east side for steamships. Lock-gates would lead from the basin to three docks, and the surrounding yards, graving docks, and slipways would be sited on reclaimed land. There would be direct rail access to the Midlands by a proposed Birmingham and central England railway. This, and other visionary plans, were abandoned when financial support was not forthcoming, and a more modest scheme was put forward by the corpor-

ation in The Harwich Improvement, Quays and Pier Act, which was passed in 1851 "despite strong and very unfair opposition from the corporation and certain shipowners of Ipswich".

Mr Peter Schuyler Bruff, an outstanding civil engineer of Ipswich, was engaged to construct a quay from the Naval Yard to King's Head Street and also a pier, officially called the Corporation Pier but known today as the Halfpenny Pier. When work began the corporation decided that "a public demonstration be made to commemorate the same, and that a procession be formed on the occasion, and that the day be made a general holiday, and that means be taken to obtain funds to provide the poor with a dinner, and also that a public dinner be held".

When the Corporation Pier opened in July, 1853, the second phase of development began with an extension of wharves of over twelve hundred feet from the pier to Bathside, on the line which the quayside still follows. Dredged material and shingle were used to reclaim land where a railway station and gasworks were subsequently built. The extent of the reclamation was considerable and completely altered the appearance of the quayside. Before 1850 the narrow, congested private quays, beginning near the present entrance to Navyard Wharf, extended from a few yards in front of the Angel and the end houses in Eastgate Street, King's Head Street and Church Street to West Street. Beyond them lay the marsh, protected by a sea wall. The old Customs House at the end of West Street was then only ten yards from the quayside. Most of the Trinity House buildings and the former Great Eastern Hotel were built on land formerly covered by the sea.

The first train arrived on 4th August, 1854, with several trucks full of navvies and the town band playing "There's a good time coming, boys"; the official opening was on 15th August, when a train left Harwich for Manningtree and the first train from London arrived. The mayor

The original station stood close to the quayside. It was demolished about 1865 to make way for cattle pens and sidings ready for the Great Eastern Railway's services from the Continental Pier.

and other distinguished guests boarded the train at Dovercourt, to be greeted at Harwich by a huge crowd out to enjoy a public holiday. On a decorated platform the band played "See the conquering hero comes", and amid long and prolonged cheers the guns at the Redoubt fired a salute. At 6 pm the mayor, John Pattrick, and about seventy others sat down to a banquet at the Three Cups, where festivities continued until a late hour. In November nearly four thousand shareholders of the ECR came from London in four special trains, each being greeted on arrival by a salvo from the guns. This time a public dinner was held on the new pier, and Ipswich supplied extra police for the day.

The first railway station was built at the seaward end of George Street on a site across the road from the present Trinity House depot.

Harwich seen from seaward in 1854 at the time the railway was opened to the town. The Naval Yard can be seen on the extreme right, St Nicholas's Church and the High Light in the middle of the picture and the Redoubt and the Low Light towards the left, with the Naze in the distance on the extreme left.

A railway line ran along the quayside to the Corporation Pier so that steamers could be bunkered from coal trucks pulled alongside by horses. Passengers walked from station to pier, which in bad weather could be a most unpleasant experience, and booked their passages at a ticket office. The scene remains much the same today except that the office was later rebuilt and given a cupola while the pier lost half its length as the result of a fire in 1927.

When the ECR took over the EUR it acquired a fleet of paddle-steamers and used the new pier for a ferry service to Ipswich. It also chartered ships from the North of Europe Steam Navigation Company and started a service from Harwich to Antwerp. Heavy losses however forced the ECR to withdraw the service after a few months. Attempts to revive it in 1855 and 1857 also failed, mainly because the vessels were too small.

Both the corporation and the ECR were soon in financial straits. The former faced heavy loan charges for the new quay and pier; the latter lost £5,976 on its shipping enterprises in the first full year, and receipts from the branch line were so low that in 1859 its closure was a possibility.

The tide turned in 1863 when the ECR was

Right: *When the construction of the Continental Pier necessitated the demolition of the original station a new one was built in what was then almost open country. This engraving by Rock & Company shows ladies enjoying a walk along the new river wall from Gashouse Creek to Dovercourt.*

Bottom right: *An advertisement for a "special cheap excursion" to London for a fare of half a crown in 1860.*

amalgamated with others to form the Great Eastern Railway, with power to expand its own shipping services at a time when political and economic developments in Europe were bringing great opportunities to British trade. Antwerp and Rotterdam assumed a new importance; the River Scheldt was opened for trade only in 1863, after being closed for two hundred years, and Bismarck was welding the German states into a great industrial power with most of its foreign trade passing through Rotterdam. The GER began a weekly service to Rotterdam in 1863 and in the following year began a similar service to Antwerp. It built the Great Eastern Hotel in what was described as "the free Italian or mixed style", where prosperous continental travellers were entertained in luxury. This enormous building was opened in July, 1865, and still stands on the quay. As it soon became apparent that the Corporation Pier was inadequate the GER constructed a new Continental Pier, now known as Trinity Pier, which opened in 1866. It was built of timber and was longer and wider than the present structure, which replaced it after a disastrous fire in 1910.

Fortunately there was an area of newly reclaimed land available for sheds, coal dumps and marshalling yards and the provision of cattle pens and water troughs for animals imported from Rotterdam, but the railway station stood in the middle of it and obstructed the approach to the new pier. The station was demolished in 1865, and a new one built on the present site.

The GER started cautiously with three chartered vessels. When these proved unsuitable the directors ordered four steamers of their own design. J. and W. Dudgeon of Cubitt Town built the first passenger ships, the paddle-steamers *Zealous* and *Avalon*, in 1864 and 1865; while G. Simpson and Company of London built two cattle boats, the *Harwich* and the *Rotterdam*, in 1864. The GER advertised its ships as "in all respects first class, the accommodation the best that can be supplied. The captains and officers are selected with the greatest possible care." It also advertised that steamers would leave Harwich on Mondays, Wednesdays and Fridays at 9 pm and arrive at Rotterdam the following morning at 8 am; returning passengers would leave Rotterdam at 9 pm and reach Harwich by 8 am. This was, to say the least, optimistic, for the sand bars on the Dutch side could be crossed only within one and a half hours of high tide, and passengers had to transfer to smaller ships so they could land without waiting for the tide to

Right: *The Great Eastern Hotel, opened in July, 1865, continued to accommodate passengers to and from the Continent until the transfer of services to Parkeston Quay in 1883.*

Opposite page: *The GER cargo steamer* Harwich *at the Corporation Pier about 1890. Built as a paddle steamer in 1864, the* Harwich *had been converted to screw propulsion in 1884.*

make. They often arrived four or five hours late and missed their connections, a situation which continued until the opening of the New Waterway.

The *Zealous* was later altered to carry freight as well as passengers, and remained in service until scrapped in 1887. The *Avalon* had a more exciting history. She was sold in 1888 and changed hands several times before being wrecked off Jamaica in 1909.

The pride of the GER fleet in its early days was the paddle-steamer *Claud Hamilton*, named after the company's popular chairman and built on the Clyde by John Elder and Company. She was launched in 1875 and was then the largest steamer built by the GER, being almost 1,000 tons and 265 feet in length. Her fine appearance and standard of accommodation did much to enhance the popularity of the Harwich route. After twenty-two years' service she was sold to the City of London for transporting cattle from Greenwich to Deptford, and dismantled in 1914.

In 1875 the *Claud Hamilton* and the *Prince of Wales* began a daily service to Rotterdam by using the New Waterway. This canal took six years to construct and was completed by the Dutch engineer Caland in 1872. It was a deep fairway from the Hook to Rotterdam capable of taking the biggest ships at all states of the tide. The first steamer to use it was a GER

Lord Claud Hamilton (1843–1925) was chairman of the Great Eastern Railway from 1892 until it was absorbed into the LNER at the grouping of 1923. In 1919 he became High Steward of Harwich.

The continental express making its way up Brentwood Bank on the way to Parkeston Quay, headed by a Claud Hamilton *class engine of the kind introduced by the Great Eastern in 1900.*

boat, the *Richard Young*, which passed through on 19th March, 1872. Times of arrival became much more reliable, and a continental express between Bishopsgate and Harwich was introduced, leaving Bishopsgate at 6 pm and arriving at Harwich at 7.53 pm. In the opposite direction, the train left Harwich at 5 am and was due in London at 7.05 am.

The use of larger ships and the increasing volume of traffic highlighted the need for a great extension of the facilities at Harwich. In 1872 the GER began to consider possible sites for development. No room existed on the Harwich peninsula in the vicinity of the quay without clearing most of the town. Such a proposal would be strongly opposed, and the chance of passing an Act forcing people to leave their homes was remote. Furthermore, during the years of new building the services would be severely disrupted.

Consideration was then given to four schemes put forward between 1845 and 1870 for the reclamation of the mudflats between Harwich and Ramsey Ray Island, but to excavate a deep-water port in such soft ground would have been difficult and very expensive. It was decided that it would be easier and cheaper to build a new quay off Ray Island, in the Stour upstream of Harwich, where there was a deep water channel, and reclaim a large area between the island and the mainland.

Plans for such a development were placed before Parliament in November, 1873, and approved in the following July. Time has shown the wisdom of the choice.

It has been suggested that the corporation imposed exorbitant rates and tolls which forced the GER to develop outside Harwich. This cannot be substantiated. A dispute did occur over the payment of a toll on coal entering Harwich, but the Act empowering the corporation to levy the charge was not directed against the GER. When it was passed in 1819 no railway existed, and at the time of the dispute in 1872 the company was already planning to move.

From 1879 to 1883 the GER carried through a vast project of reclamation and quay building. It cost over £500,000 and involved moving and using much of the high ground on Ray Island as foundations for embankments and causeways and to stabilize the marshy area of Ramsey Creek. About six hundred acres were enclosed by a sea wall which formed a curved embankment two and a half miles long. In the centre was a massive pier named Parkeston Quay after Charles H. Parkes, the chairman of GER. It was built by the Horsley Foundry Company for the sum of £67,972. Extending for 1,850 feet, it had timber decking and was supported by a thousand wooden piles. These were driven in pairs, with concrete cylinders

Right: *Parkeston Quay in the early years of this century with the cargo vessel* Colchester, *built at Hull by Earles Shipbuilding and Engineering Company in 1889, alongside the quay. In the foreground is the ill-fated* Berlin, *built by the same yard in 1894.*

Below: *When Parkeston Quay was opened in 1883 the Great Eastern laid out Hamilton Park, named after its chairman. There was an attractive walk from the village to the station.*

nine feet in diameter sunk in between. The quay provided seven berths and accommodated the station, a luxurious hotel and two large goods warehouses. To the east of the hotel were offices, and beyond them lay the Marine Shops, where maintenance work to the railway fleet was carried out, and the loco shed. Between this shed and the sea wall was an extensive cattle lairage and a licensed slaughterhouse, but outbreaks of foot and mouth disease on the Continent led to the prohibition of imports of live cattle. As the facilities were no longer required, the lairage

was pulled down in 1911 to make way for a coal stacking ground.

West of the level crossing and on the present site of the Det Forenede Dampskibs-Selskab offices were stables for ninety-six horses, many of which were at work on the quay; thirty-six more stables were built in 1914 when over ten thousand horses a year were being shipped to the Continent.

Though the loss of the continental traffic was keenly felt at Harwich, and the old port area declined, many people finding work at Parkeston Quay continued to live in the old town. While the new work was under construction the GER began to build houses for its employees on the higher ground in the middle of Ray Island. Many farm labourers came to find work and housing at Parkeston, which had a population of six hundred in 1886, rising to one thousand and sixty in 1901. It had its own school, Methodist and Anglican churches, village hall, Co-operative store, sports ground, fire station, and a supply of electricity from the

A group of Great Eastern Railway drivers, firemen and cleaners at the Parkeston "Loco" in 1904. The engine is one of James Holden's T19 class; No 752 was built at Stratford Works in 1889 and was in service until 1910, when she was scrapped.

Right: *Delivering milk in Parkeston Road in 1917. The terrace of houses on the right was built by the Great Eastern Railway in 1883 for its employees, and remained railway property until 1964.*

Below: *The youngsters of Parkeston line up for the photographer in Garland Road, named after Squire Garland, the lord of the manor.*

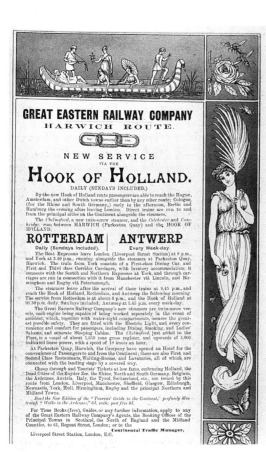

company's power station. Eight roads lay to the east of what is now called Parkeston Road; it was not until the early 1900s that houses were built on the west side. At the end of Una Road are the remains of a brickworks where Edward Saunders of Dovercourt once employed up to one hundred and fifty men making bricks and tiles. He is remembered in the name of Edward Street. Other streets, such as Hamilton, Makins and Coller, were named after directors of the GER, and Squire Garland, who was lord of the manor and had owned all the land, was commemorated by a road and a public house. Foster Road led to the factory of the Foster Manufacturing Company, where corsets were made until it became HM Customs House.

Similar developments took place on the Dutch side where a new port, linked by rail to Rotterdam, was completed at the Hook in 1893 and became the passenger terminal. This proved of great benefit to long-distance passengers, and times of sailings were more reliable when delays due to fog and other navigational hazards in the Maas could then be avoided. By a skilful and effective advertising campaign the GER made "Harwich to the Hook" known throughout England. A poster showing the chain across the sea to join the two ports was to be seen at hundreds of stations

Above left: *An ornate advertisement for the Harwich to Hook of Holland service, opened in 1893. It incorporates the chain, "the connecting link", which was to feature in later posters.*

Left and opposite page: *The Continental Pier was seriously damaged by fire on 18th June, 1910. Since the continental services had been transferred to Parkeston Quay in 1883 the pier had been used for general cargo.*

from about 1900 onwards. This was at a time when more and more of the well-to-do middle class were taking holidays abroad, and Holland enjoyed a great vogue. *Miss Hook of Holland* was a popular operetta; the music halls of 1906 rang to the strains of "By the side of the Zuyder Zee" and its innumerable parodies, polite or otherwise. Thus "business and pleasure conspired together to swell the volume of traffic through Harwich".

All this meant new and better ships, and the company replaced the paddle-steamers with a fleet of larger and more luxurious screw-propelled vessels built by the Earles Shipbuilding and Engineering Company of Hull. These were named after places connected with the company's services, beginning with the *Ipswich* and the *Norwich* in 1883, followed by the *Cambridge* (1886), *Colchester* (1889), *Chelmsford* (1893), and the *Amsterdam, Berlin* and *Vienna* in 1894. These ships gave wonderful service extending over a long period. By 1907 over 1,200,000 passengers had been carried without a single fatality, but this excellent record was tragically marred in the same year when the *Berlin* was wrecked with the loss of 128 lives in the early hours of 21st February.

A strong north-westerly gale was blowing when Captain Precious left Parkeston in the *Berlin* with over ninety passengers and a crew of fifty-one. At 5.15 am he was entering the New Waterway when a tremendous sea dashed his ship against the stone breakwater and the vessel broke in two just aft of the funnels. Most of the passengers were on the forepart, which sank quickly, and only one survivor was picked up by a lifeboat. The GER vessel *Clacton*, which had left Harwich harbour for Rotterdam shortly after the *Berlin*, was first on the scene and saw the forepart sink; she was unable to get near the wrecks which lay jammed broadside on the breakwater. Captain William Dale of the *Clacton* thought it impossible for anyone to have survived, but about twenty-five passengers and crew had taken refuge on the afterpart. A lifeboat and a pilot tug made several unsuccessful attempts to reach them; it was not until the next day that they managed to land men on the breakwater and get a line to the wreck from the beacon tower near the end of the pier. By that time there were only fifteen survivors; eleven of them slid down the rope to safety before the rising tide forced the rescuers to abandon the attempt. They had been encouraged in their efforts by Prince Henry, the Queen's consort, who was on board the tug.

It was reported that two or three women, too

The wreck of the ss Berlin *on the north pier at the Hook of Holland in 1907 was the worst disaster ever to strike the Harwich continental service. At top is the* Berlin; *above is an artist's impression of Captain Sperling's rescue of three women from the wreck; and above right is the scene as the ss Clacton arrives from Harwich and the wrecked vessel breaks in two.*

weak to use the lifeline, were still alive on the wreck. Their rescue was due to the bravery and initiative of Captain Sperling of the ss *Josephine*, who with his two nephews succeeded in reaching the iron beacon tower and climbing up the rope to the sloping deck. Close to a heap of bodies the captain found three women, each of whom he lowered to the breakwater and to safety, almost forty-eight hours after the *Berlin* had struck.

Only four of the crew survived, and there

were sad scenes as the ship bearing the recovered bodies slowly entered Harwich harbour at nightfall, while the guns of Landguard, Beacon Hill and several warships boomed out. Money poured in for the relief of the dependants, and a special fund was opened to provide the memorial in All Saints' churchyard to the chief steward, William John Moor, who had been in charge of a boy of five and was found with the dead child in his arms.

A Board of Trade inquiry found that the late master of the *Berlin* had been guilty of an error of judgement in attempting to enter the New Waterway in such conditions.

In October, 1908, Harwich was again plunged into mourning when the GER cargo steamer *Yarmouth*, under the command of Captain Avis, was lost at sea with one passenger and a crew of twenty-one. The ship left the Hook with a heavy cargo of crates of meat and three furniture vans on deck. When sighted by men on the Outer Gabbard lightship

Above: *Great Eastern Railway employees with a horse-drawn lorry at Harwich about the turn of the century.*

Left: *The cover of a guidebook in German issued by the Great Eastern Railway in connection with the Harwich–Hook service.*

Opposite page: *One of the GER steamers leaving Harwich just before the First World War.*

she was rolling heavily with a list to starboard of about forty degrees. They received no call for assistance, and the ship was soon lost in fog, never to be seen again. Fifteen of the crew were married and left twenty-nine fatherless children.

In spite of such disasters the volume of traffic continued to grow, and once again new and improved ships were needed. By 1910 all the older ships had been replaced by turbine-driven steamers equipped with the latest invention, wireless telegraphy. Each was about 2,500 tons, with cabins for most of the passengers. By using the Harwich to Hook service it was possible to reach Japan in sixteen days via the Trans-Siberian Railway.

Before the outbreak of war in 1914 the enterprise of the GER brought foreign operators to Parkeston, and services to Hamburg and Gothenburg started up though these did not survive the Great War. However, a permanent link with Denmark was forged in 1880 when the United Shipping Company, or DFDS, which had created the port of Esbjerg, made Harwich the principal port for its services to the United Kingdom. On 2nd June the 627-ton paddle-steamer *Riberhuus* arrived at Parkeston with a cargo of cattle, pigs and sheep. The original service was primarily intended for livestock only, but the *Riberhuus* had cabin space for twenty-eight, and in addition an unspecified number of hardy souls could cross the North Sea on deck. When, following an outbreak of foot and mouth disease on the Continent, the importation of live cattle was banned in 1892, Danish farmers became pig producers, and DFDS developed a system of refrigeration to bring sides of bacon for British breakfasts. As a result 28,677 tons of Danish bacon were landed at Parkeston in 1894 and then sent by rail to depots throughout the country. The first major passenger ship was introduced in 1901, and in 1913 around twenty-three thousand passengers travelled via Esbjerg.

By that time the quay had been extended westward by nine hundred feet, using concrete piling, in order to accommodate three extra berths. Facilities were improved by the installation of a new coaling plant costing nearly £10,000, a five-ton electric crane and additional warehouses. In 1895 the GER opened its own power station, which stood on the corner of Foster Road and supplied the needs of the quay until 1916, when it was demolished to make room for a garage. Extensive dredging by the Harbour Board had made it possible for larger ships to use the harbour, which was of benefit not only to merchant shipping but also to the Royal Navy. When the dredging was completed in 1910 at a cost of £40,810 the GER contributed £10,000 and the Admiralty £2,000.

Opposite page: Part of W. H. Lindsey's design for Dovercourt New Town, much of which was never built.

Below: A poster of 1815 offering a reward for information relating to what was apparently an arson attack.

The Spreading Town

5

WHEN Napoleon was banished to Elba after twenty-one years of war, poverty was widespread in Harwich, but cares were forgotten as everybody joined in the festivities to celebrate the coming of peace. The 14th July, 1814, was a day to be remembered, especially by over seven hundred poor people who sat down to a meal of roast beef and plum pudding on the Green, presided over by the mayor. "Never was the spirit of philanthropy more eminently displayed, or met with more grateful returns." In the evening, after sports and fireworks, an effigy of Napoleon in uniform was burned.

The harsh reality was that nearly all working men were paupers, eking out a miserable existence with a weekly dole which varied with the size of the family and the cost of bread. In 1776 the annual cost of poor relief in the parish of St Nicholas was £645; in 1813 it had risen to £2,538, while in the parish of Dovercourt it increased from £170 to £521 in the same period. In spite of this people were starving, and there were cases where the magistrates sent men and women to prison for twenty-one days with hard labour for stealing a few swedes from fields at Dovercourt.

Until 1836 the impotent poor found relief in the local workhouse, which the corporation had built on waste ground in 1669, but with the introduction of a new Poor Law system in 1834 the parishes of north-east Essex formed a "union", with a common workhouse and infirmary at Tendring administered by a Board of Guardians elected by adult male ratepayers.

Harwich elected three guardians, whose aim was to cut the cost of poor relief by insisting that all paupers had to enter the workhouse. Conditions were deliberately made so bad that

£.100 Reward!

WHEREAS on the Night of Saturday the fifteenth Day of July last or early the next Morning, the Ship or Breakwater, called The Empress Mary, laying on the Beach at the North extremity of Harwich, suddenly took FIRE, whereby the same sustained very considerable damage, some valuable property on board was entirely destroyed, and the adjacent Buildings at that part of the Town were alarmingly endangered.

AND Whereas upon Investigation of circumstances, there appears very strong reason to suspect and believe that the said Fire was wantonly and maliciously occasioned by some wicked and evil-disposed Person or Persons unknown: Therefore

NOTICE IS HEREBY GIVEN

That whoever will produce satisfactory Information of the Offender or Offenders in that respect, so that he or they may be brought to Justice, shall be paid a Reward of the Sum of

One Hundred Pounds

upon the Conviction of such Offender or Offenders on application to *Mr. Abraham Hindes*, Chamberlain of the Borough of Harwich aforesaid.

By Order of the Mayor and Burgesses of the said Borough.
B. CHAPMAN, *Town Clerk.*

Harwich, 5 August, 1815.

J. RAW, PRINTER, IPSWICH.

it was the last place anyone would wish to enter.

In 1836 the old workhouse was sold to the Cobbold family for conversion into a brewery, but the lack of an adequate water supply caused them to move to Ipswich in 1871 and the present vicarage was built on the site.

In Harwich the benefit of a reduced Poor Rate was offset by the imposition of a special Church Rate of four shillings in the pound towards repayment of a loan of £10,000 for rebuilding St Nicholas's Church in 1821. The council vainly petitioned Parliament to remove this burden, and pointed out the difficulties of collecting the money due to the impoverished state of the town, "and that considerable objection to the payment of any tax for the support of the Establishment is made by those who dissent from it".

Many people hoped the situation would improve after the old system of central and local government was swept away. The Reform Act of 1832 placed the election of two local MPs in the hands of adult male householders of property worth £10 a year or more, and three years later all adult male ratepayers were able to elect a council consisting of twelve councillors and four aldermen. Feeling ran high in Harwich when the first parliamentary election under the new system was held on 10th December, 1832. There was no secret ballot until 1872, and at two places in the borough temporary stages, known as the hustings, were erected where clerks openly recorded the votes. Each of the 198 voters had two votes. The Tories went in procession to one booth and the Whigs to the other to produce the following result:

Right Hon. J. C. Herries (Tory)	97
C. T. Tower (Whig)	93
N. P. Leader (Tory)	90
J. Disney (Whig)	89

In the election of 1841 the unsuccessful Whig candidate was John Bagshaw, a former East India merchant with a business in Calcutta, who settled in Harwich, took over the shipyard, and planned to build a magnificent "New Town" at Lower Dovercourt. He began in 1845 by building a mansion, Cliff House, in grounds which have since become Cliff Park, and after his election to Parliament in 1847 took an active part in bringing the railway to Harwich and passing the Harwich Improvement, Quays and Pier Act in 1851. At the same time W. H. Lindsey, a London architect, produced plans and drawings of "Dover Court New Town, Essex", and when a chalybeate spring was discovered in the grounds of Cliff House

Left: *The entrance hall to Cliff House, John Bagshaw's mansion, closely resembled the hall of the Great Eastern Hotel, built nearly twenty years later.*

Opposite above: *John Bagshaw was a man of many parts. He built ships at the Naval Yard from 1840 to 1851, became Member of Parliament in 1847 and planned Dovercourt New Town.*

Opposite page: *Cliff House, built in 1845 and demolished in 1909.*

Bagshaw built the Spa, which opened in 1854 and incorporated a pump room, reading room and library. Dovercourt was set to rival Brighton and Tunbridge Wells. The *Essex Standard* of 31st July, 1856, reported:

> Visitors of Dovercourt Spa
> The Earl of Stradbroke, the Duke of Wellington, Lord Stanley, Sir Fitzroy Kelly, and his friends, with the Honorable William Beresford, came by the *Atlanta* steamer, specially engaged for the occasion, from Ipswich and left after visiting the town and Spa.

The first building was Orwell Terrace, which gives some idea of what the whole town might have looked like. Bagshaw's son Robert took up residence at Banksea House at the seaward end in 1857. The slopes from Orwell Terrace to Mill Lane were landscaped, with a grotto, shelters and a miniature waterfall that fed a pool large enough to accommodate a pair of swans, but this cost over £10,000, and John Bagshaw was in financial difficulties. He completed the construction of Marine Parade and laid out what he called the Cliff Estate, but he was adjudged bankrupt in 1859. He died in Norwood in 1861 after the contents of his house and the Spa had been sold and his extensive estate broken up. After remaining empty for some years Cliff House was de-

molished in 1909; eleven years later the Spa suffered a similar fate at the hands of the corporation, and Orwell Terrace is now John Bagshaw's chief memorial.

Robert Bagshaw, who also became MP for Harwich, developed Victoria Street in 1864. Ten years later he built the Evangelical Church in what was then a new road called Stour Road, before it was paved and sewered in 1903 and named Kingsway. For some years preachers from the Evangelisation Society had been allowed to use Bagshaw's Assembly Rooms, which stood in Orwell Road and could seat about two hundred. These proved to be inadequate and he engaged Gibbons of Ipswich to design a hall for seven hundred at a cost of £2,500. In the vestibule Robert Bagshaw placed a memorial stone to his mother and sister, who had been drowned in the River Hooghly in 1820. The church was sold in 1985 for conversion into a "mini-market".

Following John Bagshaw's bankruptcy Beadel and Sons of London sold twenty-five acres of his estate for building-sites, mainly along Marine Parade, Cliff Road, Fronks Road and in adjoining fields. They advertised the sale in glowing terms:

It is seldom that so advantageous an opportunity offers for Investment as the present. The Villa Residences already completed—the great extent of direct frontage to the Sea—the convenience of access by Rail—the clean sandy beach—elevated position—extent and beauty of scenery—proximity to the Town of Harwich, and the increasing demand in this locality for Marine Residences render this Property eminently attractive.

By arrangement with the Eastern Counties Railway Company occupiers of Houses built before the 15th August, 1861, of the annual value of £50 and upwards, are entitled to Concessions from the Company for a term of 20 years for travelling on their line, between London and Dovercourt, with the option of stopping at one intermediate station, at an annual charge of £20.

Local Steamers run continually between Harwich and Ipswich on the picturesque River Orwell.

Harwich enjoys the advantage of Two Postal Deliveries from the Metropolis daily.

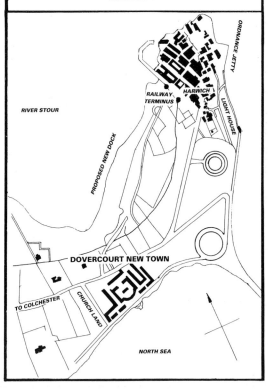

DOVER COURT NEW TOWN, ESSEX.
the Property of John Bagshaw Esqre
TO LET
ON BUILDING LEASES
For Particulars Apply to
CHA^s. S. DUNCAN ARCH.^T
72. LOMBARD S^T CITY

Some of this estate was bought by Henry Lee and Son, builders, who celebrated the start of work on Cliff Terrace with a dinner for forty employees at the Victoria Hotel in February, 1861. Progress was very slow, and they had built only the terrace and two houses in Lee Road before going bankrupt in 1882. They sold out to the Chelmsford Land Company, which continued building in Lee Road and developed First, Second and Third Avenues.

Before Bagshaw's bankruptcy, Trinity House had reserved a site in Fronks Road "for

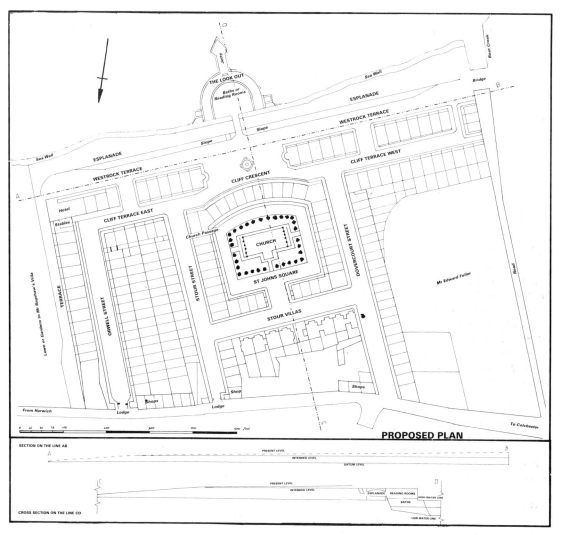

PROPOSED PLAN

SECTION ON THE LINE AB

CROSS SECTION ON THE LINE CD

the purpose of erecting a Light House or Light Houses, with light-keepers' dwelling, store-house, and other buildings thereon", while T. Daniel and Son, brewers of West Bergholt, had acquired the site for the Cliff Hotel.

The orchard and meadow in the top right-hand corner of the map on pages 48 and 49 was bought by Mr J. E. A. Gwynne, a civil engineer of London, and developed as the Clifton Estate, comprising Waddesdon Road, Gwynne Road and Grafton Road. From 1871 to 1878 he resided at Cliff House.

The map shows the growth of the shopping area about 1860. In the eighteen-nineties shops were built in front of the new terrace of houses on the north side of the new High Street, which, with fine shops on the south, eventually reached the present Kingsway. On one corner of the crossroads Mr G. W. Smith opened his greengrocer's shop in 1898. Four years later the local Co-operative Society, Mr E. C. Pattinson, draper, and the Capital and Counties Bank opened premises on the other corner sites.

The first shops of Bagshaw's "new town" ran along Dovercourt High Street from Orwell Road to the Queen's Hotel and then continued as far as Woodward's, the chemists, seen at centre right in this photograph taken about 1900. On the other side of the street can be seen the King's Arms, another early Bagshaw development, belonging to "Dick" Appleby.

By 1914 both sides of the High Street were lined with shops from Orwell Road to Kingsway, only one private house remaining in this stretch. On the left can be seen the Capital and Counties Bank, built in 1902; the Eastern Drug Company, later incorporated in Lloyd's Bank premises; and the Continental Cafe, with its enormous advertisement flag.

Looking the other way along High Street, we see the King's Arms on the right and, across Victoria Street, Mr Harryot's Temperance Hotel, with its advertisements for Cadbury's cocoa in the windows. On the left, with large white lamps, is Hunter's boot and clothing stores.

G. W. Smith, market gardener, built his shop at the junction of High Street and Stour Road, now called Kingsway, in 1898. This was purpose built as a shop; other buildings in High Street were originally private houses but later lost their bay windows when shops were built out into the front gardens.

Below: *The shops shown here filled the vacant site visible on the right of the upper picture on the opposite page. In the middle is Greenwood's butcher's shop, built in 1903, and on the right is Thompson's "model stores" of 1900.*

Left: *The garden of Banksea House, the home of Robert Bagshaw, as it was in 1876.*

Bottom of page: *W. H. Lindsey's perspective view of Dovercourt New Town. The plan was impressive, but only Orwell Terrace, seen on the right of the picture, was actually built.*

The demand for houses was steady, especially after Parkeston Quay opened in 1883, and at a time when the railway was the chief form of transport proximity to the station was of prime importance to developers as the new town expanded in a westerly direction. It grew in a piecemeal fashion as leases of manorial land expired and copyhold was converted to freehold before being sold.

The map of 1864 shows an early example of residential development on former manorial land lying to the south of the High Street as it began to extend westwards up the hill beyond Kingsway. Here the street named after the Reverend William Hordle, the popular minister of the Independent Chapel in George Street, was begun in 1869, and a terrace of cottages joined Hordle Place to another in Mill Lane. The changes in land-level in this vicinity are due to the old brickfields.

On the north side of the High Street there was very little development, for wealthy men had built mansions on the hill overlooking the Stour. One of them was Holly Lodge, built by Thomas Cobbold in 1821 and demolished in 1983 when a new telephone exchange was erected on the site. The new road to the station cut across its grounds.

On the field adjoining Holly Lodge on its western side Mr Gwynne began to build the Hill Estate in 1874. It included the terrace on the High Street, and extended from the National School, which opened in that year, to the new Hill Road. Here he gave land on which St Augustine's Church was built in 1884. He felt a church was necessary "to supply the wants of the population which is being brought to Lower Dovercourt by the building of large docks at Parkeston".

Westward from Hill Road was Hill House,

Right: *Orwell Terrace as it was about the turn of the century. The rough ground in the foreground is the site of a brickyard.*

Below: *Kingsway in the early years of this century, showing the campanile of the Kingsway Mission Hall, built by Robert Bagshaw in 1874. On the left is the Alexandra Hotel.*

now called Mill House, which was the home of John Pattrick, an alderman and mayor of Harwich. In his affidavit of 1855 he described himself as "a cement manufacturer, coal merchant, malster, miller, corn merchant, brick maker and other trades and businesses". His father moved to Harwich from Thorpe le Soken in 1809 and took the lease of the windmill and granary, which John bought in 1829. The map of 1864 shows the house which he built in 1820, with stables and business premises near to the mill. On charts it was usually called Pattrick's Mill to distinguish it

from Dovercourt Mill which from time immemorial had stood on the cliff overlooking Mill Bay at the end of Mill Lane, until coastal erosion caused it to become unsafe. It was taken down in 1829 to be re-erected in 1835 on the site shown on the same map, near to the present junction of Fronks Road and Marine Parade. The erosion had been caused by the removal of stone from the cliff to be converted into cement by John Pattrick at the extensive works indicated in the top left-hand corner of the map. To transport the bricks and tiles that he made he dredged a channel to a wharf, but

45

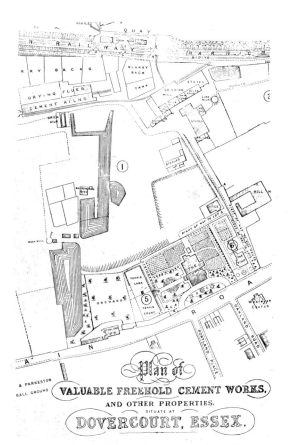

A sale plan of J. R. Pattrick's cement works at Dovercourt. At the time of the sale in 1906 all the land between Main Road and the River Stour, with the exception of the Royal Oak, belonged to Pattrick.

the coming of the railway cut off part of the access, and Pattrick claimed compensation from the Eastern Union Railway. Eventually the EUR had to fill in the old dock and build a new quay.

People living in the vicinity regarded him as a nuisance. As an alderman he was present at the council meeting on 10th February, 1869, when a petition was received from inhabitants complaining that they were "seriously affected by pestilential effluvia and smoke arising from the Portland Cement Works" and asking for action to be taken to abate the nuisance, which they believed was prejudicial to health. They had good grounds for their fears as four people who lived in cottages near the works had died in 1862 from gas from the kilns. Mr Gwynne took Pattrick to court in 1871 and forced him to build a chimney shaft 320 feet high. It remained a feature of the skyline until the outbreak of war in 1939.

After the death of John Pattrick in 1872 his son John Robson Pattrick left his two un-married sisters at Hill House and moved in 1885 to the Tower, which he built next door. By that time the cement industry in Harwich was dying, and in 1906 the whole estate was sold. Pattrick moved into The Villa, which stood adjacent to the Tower on the corner of Pattrick's Lane. The quay and works were bought by Groom and Sons, the timber mer-chants, while the Tower was acquired by Mr E. M. Jackson and remained a boarding school for boys until 1914, when it became a military hospital; the school moved to Mistley.

Meanwhile there had been some develop-ment on land between Main Road and the sea. When Bagshaw's land was sold some houses had already been built in Cliff Road to house the families and servants of the well-to-do. This continued, and other large houses were built along Main Road on land facing the grounds of Hill House. One of these was Hillcrest, which bears the date 1898 and is now the offices of the solicitors Hanslip Ward and Company. It was built by Edward Saunders, an alderman and mayor from 1912 to 1918, and at the rear were his yard and workshops. His Hillcrest Estate included Brooklyn and Oak-land Roads, and the site for the Wesleyan Methodist Church which opened in 1905.

With the coming of the motor car it was possible to live at a greater distance from the station, and Saunders began to extend Fronks Road beyond Beach Road. Fine, large houses were built on the seaward side, mainly for pilots, civil servants, businessmen and man-agerial staff associated with Parkeston Quay, so that by 1914 the quiet leafy thoroughfare

Right: *At the beginning of the century, when this photograph was taken, "The Lane" usually meant what is now Wick Lane and Low Road, while "The Lanes" in the plural was what is now Fronks Road.*

Below: *When this photograph was taken in 1907 Fronks Road had been made up and paved as far as Elmhurst Road and developers were beginning to push westward along "The Lanes", which were to be widened three years later.*

called The Lanes had been widened and transformed into the Fronks Road of today.

It was around 1910 that the first houses were built on the Main Road to the west of the Tower, on land facing the County High School. This was part of Blue House Farm and belonged to Mr G. W. Smith, who lived at a house called The Vine and grew produce to sell in his shops in Market Street, Harwich, and High Street, Dovercourt.

When the outbreak of war caused a temporary halt to housebuilding, the new town had almost linked up with a much earlier development on a strip of manorial land extending from the manor house in Manor Lane to Main Road, which Mr G. L. Jackson, a Harwich printer, bought in 1879. After he had built the terraces in what he called Manor House Road, sporadic building took place as sites became available along Main Road, until by 1914 it extended as far as the junction with Fronks Road and the old part of the borough, now called Upper Dovercourt.

When Bagshaw began his new town Dovercourt was a village of about fifty cottages. Some stood on the Green, others were near the Trafalgar Inn and in the vicinity of All Saints' Church. In 1911 a terrace of houses was built on the south side of the road facing the Green, followed by others in Clarke's Road, but as the village was a long way from the nearest railway station the demand for houses was small before 1914. A few were built at the western end of the Green near the tollhouse and gate, where road users paid for the upkeep of the turnpike until 1866 when R. J. Bagshaw, who owned Tollgate Farm, bought the house for £25 and demolished it; there was no development beyond this point.

The new Co-operative Society bought Tollgate Farm in 1885 and rented Vicarage Farm and High House Farm to set up a large dairy business; in 1913 however it gave up farming and obtained supplies elsewhere. Although growth was slow the population of the parish of All Saints more than doubled between 1871 and the end of the century, and in 1901 numbered 3,894. The parish extended from

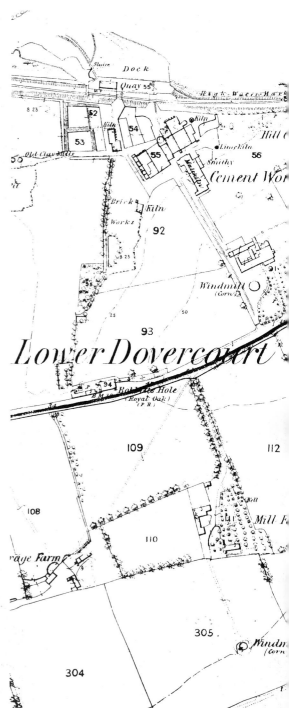

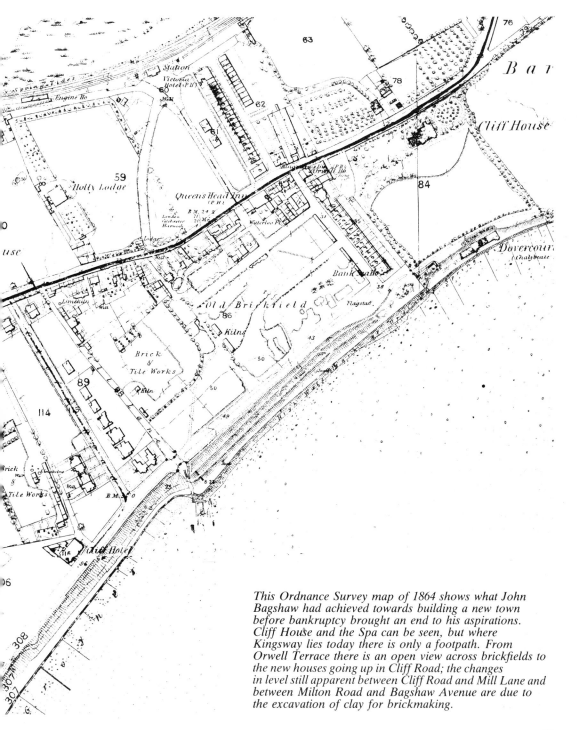

This Ordnance Survey map of 1864 shows what John Bagshaw had achieved towards building a new town before bankruptcy brought an end to his aspirations. Cliff House and the Spa can be seen, but where Kingsway lies today there is only a footpath. From Orwell Terrace there is an open view across brickfields to the new houses going up in Cliff Road; the changes in level still apparent between Cliff Road and Mill Lane and between Milton Road and Bagshaw Avenue are due to the excavation of clay for brickmaking.

Gipsy Lane, some 250 yards west of the Tollgate, to Main Road School in the east, where the boundary is marked by a stone bearing the borough arms at the foot of the gatepost. In the adjoining parish of St Nicholas another "new town" had arisen.

Harwich in 1851 was described as "the most densely populated town in the county", with an average of six persons to a dwelling. What had once been gardens were now covered with houses in yards where the sun never shone, sanitation was primitive and most people drank rain water. With the coming of the railway and the Great Eastern Railway steamers the demand for houses increased, and developers turned their attention to what was once Harwich Marsh. This area, lying between the railway and the Stour, was protected by a sea wall built during the earlier reclamation work. It was here, soon after 1860, that the United Land Company of Chelmsford planned to build "the new town of Harwich on Bathside"; in 1873 work began in Maria Street, followed by Coke Street, Pepys Street, Canning Street, Stour Street and Station Road. The population of the parish of St Nicholas rose from 3,839 in 1861 to 6,176 in 1901, bringing new problems and responsibilities for a corporation not anxious to face them.

Opposite page: *This map of Harwich in 1890 shows the grid pattern of a medieval town with the roads to the quays running parallel to each other. By 1890 the gardens and orchards of fine town houses had been filled with tenements packed within the old town walls.*

1 Treadwheel crane
2 The Naval Yard
3 Corporation Pier
4 Great Eastern Hotel
5 Continental Pier
6 Grooms' timber yard
7 Site of first railway station
8 Custom House
9 Site of Salvation Army Naval and Military Home
10 Wesleyan Methodist Chapel
11 White Hart Hotel
12 Canns' shipyard
13 Site of Bathside Battery
14 Bathside new town
15 New railway station
16 Ordnance Building
17 Guard room (now a public convenience)
18 Site of eighteenth-century baths
19 Bathside Independent Chapel
20 Government House
21 Primitive Methodist Chapel
22 Esplanade School
23 Guildhall
24 Three Cups Hotel
25 Dead-house and fire station
26 Vicarage
27 Corporation School
28 Harwich Bank
29 Angel Gate coastguard station
30 Angel Gate Battery
31 Baths, 1843, and first RHYC clubhouse
32 Market
33 A typical block, demolished in the nineteen-fifties save for the Wellington Inn.

Milk being delivered to a cottage in Wick Lane, near the present Kreswell Grove, about 1910. The milk came from Lodge Farm, which covered a large area to the east of Hall Lane.

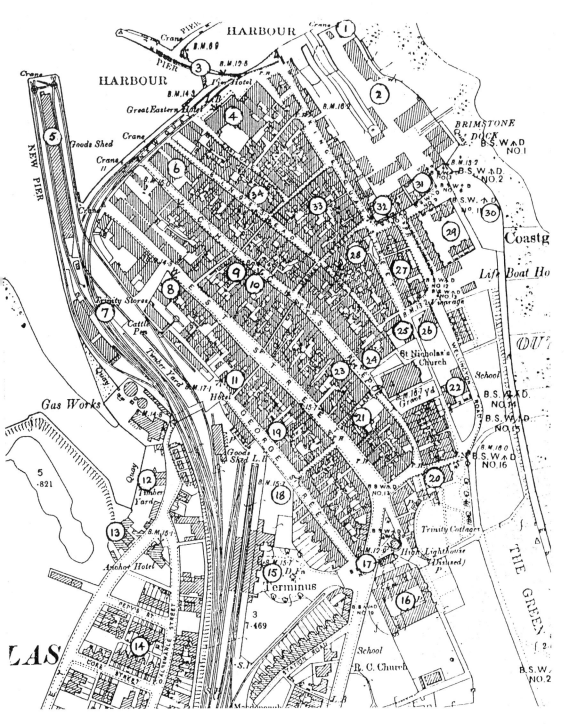

HARBOUR

HARBOUR

PIER

NEW PIER

Crane

B.M.8.9

B.M.12.8

B.M.14.3

Pier Hotel

Great Eastern Hotel

Goods Shed

Crane

Crane

Crane

Crane

BRIMSTONE DOCK

B.S.W.A.D NO.1

B.M.13.7

B.S.W.A.D NO.2

B.S.W.A.D NO.1

B.S.W.A.D NO.12

B.M.13.7

Coastg

Life Boat Ho

St Nicholas's Church

School

Anchorage

B.S.W.A.D NO.14

B.S.W.A.D NO.15

Trinity Stores

Cattle Pen

Timber Yard

B.M.17.1

Hotel

B.M.14.8

Quay

Gas Works

5
·821

Timber Yard

Goods Shed L.I.

B.M.15.7

B.M.15.1

B.M.16.0

B.S.W.A.D NO.16

Trinity Cottages

High Lighthouse (Disused)

B.S.W.A.D NO.13

B.S.W.A.D NO.9

Anchor Hotel

B.M.15.7

Terminus

3
7.469

School

R. C. Church

B.S.W.A NO.2

LAS

THE GREE

OU

St Nicholas's Church

Grove

Pro Bono Publico   6

A PETITION by the council to the Lords of the Treasury in 1812 mentioned "many and considerable public grievances", the chief ones being "the want of fresh and wholesome water, the want of proper paving and lighting of streets, and the repairing or rebuilding of the parish church". In November, 1818, a meeting in the Guildhall was called at the request of many leading citizens to see what might be done to improve things. The mayor, John Hopkins, took the chair, and it was decided to proceed by a private Act of Parliament, entitled "An Act for Paving, Cleansing, Lighting, Watching and otherwise improving the Town of Harwich, and for supplying it with Water", with commissioners empowered to raise a rate. Of the eighteen commissioners, sixteen were members of the council, and the mayor was always chairman. They appointed Mr William Scott as surveyor, and plans were drawn up in consultation with Mr (later Sir) William Cubitt, an eminent civil engineer and consultant to Ransomes of Ipswich. The first job was to pave footpaths with York flagstones to replace the soft stone collected from the shore, and work began in Mr Hopkins's lane, leading from his house in King's Head Street to Church Street.

Porches, steps, railings and anything else which projected into pavements were removed; streets which had also been made of soft local stone were taken up and brick drains were laid down the centre, with connecting drains made of brick or tree trunks to serve some properties. Salt water was used for watering streets, flushing sewers and lavatories, and in 1856 a lavatory was installed in the Free School in King's Quay Street; but most houses were served by earth closets or cesspools, emptied by scavengers who paid for the privilege of selling the contents to local farmers. The drains emptied into the sea.

The town was lit by about thirty oil lamps, and it was resolved "that the ancient names of the streets, lanes and passages be inserted at every corner thereof throughout the town". Good examples of old cast-iron plates may be seen in West Street, Church Street, King's Quay Street and Golden Lion Lane, and a particularly interesting one in George Street reads OUTER PART OF TOWN WESTWARD.

Attempts made in 1820 to find a supply of wholesome water proved unsuccessful. A test boring, described as being in front of the theatre in West Street, reached a depth of 356 feet before being abandoned. Although many wells existed, some in dangerous proximity to privies and cesspools, most people continued to rely on rainwater collected in their cellars in cisterns called rainbacks and pumped by hand to the kitchen.

The commissioners levied a rate of ninepence in the pound on householders and a toll of two shillings per cauldron on coal entering Harwich, and when the council took over their powers in 1836 the streets of the town had been greatly improved. Yet there were pressing problems of public health, mainly due to bad sanitation, polluted water, overcrowding and

53

bad housing, which brought outbreaks of typhus, smallpox, tuberculosis and the dreaded Indian cholera. The council and many inhabitants were loth to take action which would lead to a rise in rates but were forced to do so by legislation. Thus in 1855 a part-time Sanitary Inspector was appointed at £10 a year, but an inspector from the Medical Department of the Privy Council reported that from a sanitary point of view Harwich was in a dangerous condition. Sewage released in front of the quay at Harwich and Mr Bagshaw's drain down Victoria Street which discharged into the river near the station were particularly offensive and invited further outbreaks of cholera. Following an epidemic in 1866 the council ordered Bagshaw to do something about the problem in Victoria Street. He refused to do anything, and that was the end of it. Similarly, complaints

about "the pestilential effluvia" from Pattrick's cement works were ignored.

In 1871, however, the council was instructed to join with Ipswich in setting up a Joint Cholera Committee which would take precautions against the disease and provide a hospital. Until then no accommodation had been available locally for victims. As a result two ships were bought for £60 and moored off Shotley. The larger one, *The Sisters*, was fitted up as a hospital, and *The Sara* kept in reserve, with a man and his wife in charge full time at twelve shillings a week. Dr Freshfield received one guinea for each visit to the ships and two guineas for attending each case of cholera.

Following a Public Health Act in 1872 and four deaths from typhoid fever the following year, the council appointed Dr Freshfield as Medical Officer of Health and Mr Henry

White Hart Lane seen from George Street in 1933, with the entrance to the White Hart Hotel on the left. It was an example of the medieval lanes, staggered to break the force of the cold easterly winds, that ran from east to west across the peninsula.

Ditcham as Surveyor and Inspector of Nuisances. They were also paid to work for the Port Sanitary Authority set up in 1873 to supervise health arrangements in ships, the examination of passengers and the inspection of meat. A similar body was set up at Ipswich. The Joint Cholera Committee was then disbanded in the same year and the hospital ships were sold.

The new Public Health Committee reported to the council in 1874 that it had received many complaints from Mr Gwynne, the United Land Company and other developers regarding the lack of sewers; many privies were overflowing because the farmers who usually emptied them were too busy to do so; the situation was aggravated by the hot summer, which had caused a grave water shortage. The Committee urged that action should be taken "in order to avoid litigation and trouble, which are certain to follow any neglect on the part of the Council", so the council bought a cart and two horses for the collection of refuse, which was deposited on land hired from Luke Richmond at Dovercourt for £11 a year.

This did not satisfy Mr Gwynne, who threatened legal action and complained to the Local Government Board; they advised the council to consult a competent engineer. Mr Peter Bruff was appointed advisor on sanitary matters and drew up a scheme for sewering the borough. This was rejected in 1876 after a public meeting had been called to express the opposition of the inhabitants, and it was not until May, 1879, that the council agreed to borrow £10,000 for drainage works. The first sewer ran down Main Road from the newly built Isolation Hospital to a pumping station in Fernlea Road, and across War Department land to an outfall at the end of the stone breakwater. Two years later in 1882 it was extended along Main Road as far as the new vicarage. However, until the houses were served with water the sewers were not adequately flushed and could be very offensive. In 1908 the main sewer was extended for another mile beyond Manor Road, though the Upper Dovercourt area was not properly drained until 1946, when new works were built at Brookman's Farm on the shore adjacent to the Dovercourt Caravan Camp.

The Isolation Hospital was built after an outbreak of smallpox in November, 1879, brought by a person from London who died from the disease. Within a month, after seventeen fresh cases had appeared, four of them fatal, it was decided to build a hospital; as a temporary measure nine new houses in Vansittart Street were rented for a year and furnished to accommodate the thirty-four patients in the charge of Dr Sall and Nurse Luard. This proved effective, for no cases of smallpox were admitted when the hospital opened in 1880 on the site next to the Royal Oak football ground.

The report of the Public Health Committee regarding the appointment of a caretaker reads like a passage from the Old Testament:

> And they have agreed with Lot and his wife to take charge of the Building and to do all that is necessary therein, and it is further provided that Lot shall take charge of the said Land and all premises thereon, as well as the Hospital, also other property there belonging to the Corporation, and especially that he shall look after the horses belonging to the Corporation on Sundays, and further that he shall otherwise employ his time under the direction of the Surveyor, and that for such services of Lot and his wife they are to be entitled to reside on the premises and to be found with coal and to be paid at the rate of 15/- per week.

The hospital was used mainly for cases of scarlet fever and diphtheria until 1938, when patients were sent to Colchester and the premises used as a corporation depot.

The bricks for the buildings were made on site, and when the work was completed 312,000 surplus bricks were sold off at twenty-four shillings and sixpence per hundred. Laid out to a typical pavilion plan of the day, the building stood as a rare example of a Victorian isolation hospital until its demolition in 1989.

As the number of new houses in the borough steadily grew so the need for a supply of pure water became more acute. Water for Bagshaw's "new town" was taken from large, deep, brick-built wells on land near the High Street, between the King's Arms and Waddesdon Road, and stored in a great tank, but in 1890 it was found to be unfit for human consumption. Mr Bruff made an agreement with the council to provide a supply, and in 1865 he laid pipes to take water from a well at Brookman's Farm; this also proved to be impure. It was clear that the council would have to look outside Harwich for a satisfactory

The Groom drinking fountain at the junction of West Street and Wellington Road proved something of a hazard to traffic; its destruction in 1946 was probably no accident.

supply. Bruff took a leading part in setting up the Tendring Hundred Waterworks Company in 1884, which after a good deal of haggling over the cost finally brought fresh wholesome water to the borough in 1887, the year of Queen Victoria's Golden Jubilee.

It was some time before all houses could be connected to the mains, and at first people drew supplies from a standpipe at the end of West Street. Here in 1904 a drinking fountain with troughs for horses and dogs was erected, funded by surplus contributions for a portrait in oils of Alderman William Groom. It was an imposing edifice, described in *The Harwich and Dovercourt Newsman* as having "the general shape of an obelisk, about 20 feet in height, with battlemented angles surmounted by a tapered spire and a gas lamp". As the years went by its position, in the middle of the road at the junction of West Street and Wellington Road, made it a traffic hazard, and few motorists regretted its disappearance in 1946 when in the early hours of a Sunday morning it was reduced to a heap of rubble by an explosion which was probably no accident.

The water tower, the iron structure in Fronks Road, came into use in 1903 because it had proved difficult to maintain a satisfactory supply in what was the highest part of the borough. Some of the new, larger houses had bathrooms, but this was a luxury denied to most people before the Second World War and they usually had a weekly wash in a portable bath, made of zinc or tin, filled with hot water from the scullery boiler. The corporation did not provide public baths, but after 1912 it was possible to have a hot bath at the new Naval and Military Home which the Salvation Army built in Church Street. This was demolished in 1987.

The United Land Company pressed the council to take over the new streets on Bathside, but it refused until they had been made up to a satisfactory standard. The first to be adopted was Albemarle Street in 1883; it was lit by gas lamps which since 1870 had replaced the old oil lamps.

The Harwich Gas and Coke Company paid

Right: *An imposing gas lamp in Cliff Road, Dovercourt, in the first decade of this century.*

Below: *Another gas lamp of more standard design in Dovercourt High Street about 1912.*

£550 in 1854 for reclaimed land and a wharf on Bathside. Its engineer, Mr Jabez Church, built the works and gasometer there which remained until 1965. It was an ideal situation for bringing in supplies of coal by sea from the north-east and taking away coke and tar. However the provision of gas proved to be a slow business, and it was not until 1882 that Main Road was lit as far as the Isolation Hospital. One cause for delay was that when the terms for supplying gas were reviewed every three years the council invariably found the charges to be excessive. In 1891 it returned to the use of oil lamps until this became more expensive and a new contract was made with the gas company. Crompton and Company Limited of Chelmsford were consulted on the possibility of lighting Harwich by electricity, and in 1899 the council gave permission for the Harwich Electric Lighting and Tramways Company Limited to lay tramlines from Harwich Quay up Church Street, Main Road, Cliff Road, Marine Parade, and along Fronks Lane to the top of Beach Road. Both these schemes came to nothing, and the lamplighter continued to go round at dusk and dawn with a long pole, for turning the gas on or off, until 1924, when the council provided electricity, taking its supply from the London and North Eastern Railway power station at Parkeston. Half the initial cost

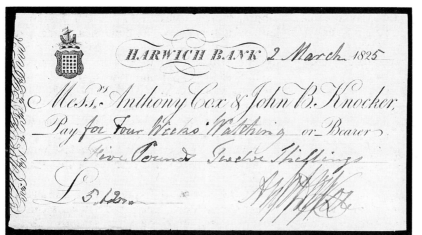

A cheque for £5 12s signed by Anthony Cox, treasurer to the Paving Commissioners, "for Four Weeks' Watching" in 1825. It is drawn on the Harwich Bank, set up in 1780 by Charles Cox, Anthony's father, who was six times Mayor of Harwich.

of £27,578 for equipment was paid by the Unemployment Grants Committee; the scale of unemployment at the time can be judged from the fact that 223 people applied for the job of Electrical Engineer. The post, which attracted a salary of £400 a year, went to Mr E. Jordan.

The necessity for a system of public lighting and keeping watch in Harwich was appreciated by the commissioners responsible under the Act of 1819, for in the succeeding years they had good reason to fear the starving masses. Part-time constables were employed, but no regular watch was kept by night until 1824, when it was reported:

> In consequence of the alarming fire on Sunday last at the dwelling houses in Church Street belonging to the Misses Clements and others, the act of some incendiary at present unknown, several persons, . . . on behalf of themselves and others, have voluntarily offered gratuitously to watch the Town through the Winter.

This offer was accepted, and from a sum of £66 17s raised by voluntary subscriptions the commissioners were able to enrol ten watchmen. Two of them were paid two shillings each per night to patrol the streets between 10 pm and 6 am, and a third was paid one shilling per week "for watching the streets during the evening and keeping an eye on boys who frequent the same", but this ended when the

fund was exhausted. In 1830, however, strikes and riots erupted in the industrial centres, and agricultural uprisings were on a far larger scale than any which had occurred before. Around Oakley labourers destroyed the threshing machines and other new implements that reduced the demand for labour, and the ricks of unpopular farmers went up in flames, but there was no loss of life in what proved to be the last of the great outbreaks of disorder. At a special meeting held on 8th December, 1830, it was resolved that "owing to the present disturbed state of the country, it is found expedient to appoint suitable persons as night watchmen for the protection of the Town".

A step towards the establishment of a regular police force was taken in 1836, when as a result of the Municipal Corporations Act the council set up a Watch Committee. It appointed William Burton, the gaoler, as Chief Constable at a salary of £20 per annum. He was required "to be always on duty during the day to preserve the peace of the Borough, and to prevent the frequent interruptions and stoppages occasioned by persons standing at the corners of the streets". The force consisted of nine constables at Harwich and three at Dovercourt, all working part-time. Their regular duties were to patrol places of worship on Sundays and public houses on Saturday nights for a fee of two shillings and one shilling respectively. For working longer hours in the execution of his duty a constable could be paid up to three shillings and sixpence a day, but this was found to be insufficient when escorting prisoners to Springfield Gaol, and the following scale was adopted:

> For 1 prisoner, 10d a mile;
> 2 prisoners, 7d each per mile;
> 3, or more, prisoners, 6d each per mile;
> 5/- per day, and 2/6d per night for loss of time;
> 1/- per day, and 1/6d per day and night, for the sustenance of each prisoner during such conveyance.

A policeman's lot was not always a happy one, as Thomas Wilding found out in August, 1837, when he received severe injuries in apprehending a deserter from Her Majesty's surveying brig *Fairy*. The council agreed to pay the surgeon's bill of £4 9s 6d, together with a payment to Wilding of £1 per week for four weeks' loss of time and "the sum of £1 as a gratuity for his activity". This seems to be fairly generous, possibly because the Admiralty was expected to meet the bill. In 1841 Constable Joseph Meachen received only £1 compensation when he injured his eye and lost his hat in an affray with some soldiers at the King's Head.

On the advice of Captain John McHardy, Chief Constable of Essex, the council set up a regular force in Harwich in January, 1848, consisting of Police constables Rush, Moore

A top-hatted policeman stands on duty outside the Guildhall, which housed the police station until the building of a new one in Main Road in 1913–15. The Harwich Borough Police amalgamated with the county constabulary in 1857.

and Slater and Superintendent George Coleman. The constables were paid eighteen shillings per week plus a shoe allowance of one shilling and sixpence, while their chief received twenty-five shillings per week, less £8 per annum for his accommodation on the top floor of the Guildhall. The first uniforms of top hats, frock coats and trousers were supplied by Clarke of Ipswich for £26 19s.

The Guildhall became the police headquarters, and the ground floor was converted to offices. New cells were built in the yard at the rear; the office of gaoler was abolished, and the Bridewell, which had served as a gaol for minor offences, was converted into a dwelling.

Relations between the council and Superintendent Coleman soon became strained. When he reported Pc Slater for getting married while on leave, without previously obtaining permission, he was informed that "the marriage was not considered an offence against the regulations" and that he should call the attention of his men to orders regarding "talking and walking with people, and going into Public Houses or drinking therein during the time of duty". Finally the Harwich Police Force merged with the Essex Constabulary, and on 1st February, 1857, Inspector Banks took charge with two sergeants and four constables. It took some time for the Watch Committee and magistrates to accept the fact that they no longer had any jurisdiction over Inspector Banks, and the Chief Constable had to come and explain the situation in October, 1858, when Alderman Vaux, JP, was very angry because his order that a boy should be locked up had not been obeyed. Strong dissatisfaction was felt by many that constables no longer carried canes and were unable to deal with naughty boys as they did in earlier days.

It is surprising that nothing was done until 1858 to guard against the growing danger of fire in crowded yards and narrow lanes where many tenements were constructed of wood. In that year the Vestry of St Nicholas bought a large and a small steam fire engine from Shand,

Opposite page: *Members of the Harwich Fire Brigade photographed about 1916 with David Wills, chairman of the Fire Brigade Committee and honorary captain of the brigade, sitting in the middle of the front row. He was a baker and confectioner in Church Street.*

Right: *The brigade's equipment, including a Shand Mason steam fire engine on the right, in the Corporation fire station built in 1912.*

Mason and Company of London, which they asked the council to maintain, but they were informed that it had no power to do so. Fourteen years later, with nothing done to them, the engines were reported to be "greatly out of order and unfit for use", and the council took them over in 1873. On the advice of the makers the small engine, which was beyond repair, was replaced by a second-hand engine from the London Fire Brigade, while the large engine was overhauled. Until 1915 horses were hired to pull the engine, but the council then bought two horses of its own for £50. In an emergency additional help was given by the army, the navy and the Great Eastern Railway brigade from Parkeston. This arrangement lasted until 1925, when the council sold the horses and bought a Dennis motor fire engine for £960. An engine house, stables and a dead-house, or mortuary, were built and may still be seen to the rear of the Three Cups. Following the destruction by fire of houses and other corporate property in 1911 a site was cleared for a new fire station and Station Officer's house, the Palace cinema and a public convenience.

The brigade comprised eighteen men, all serving on a part-time basis except for Station Officer Mills. He was appointed in 1914 at twenty-five shillings a week with free accommodation, light and coal, and told that "his duties consist of cleaning the Surveyor's offices and the public lavatory, and the remainder of the day at the Fire Station". A very interesting job. At that time the Borough Engineer and Surveyor had his offices in the adjacent old Corporation School. The convenience still stands on the Wellington Road corner of the site.

When war broke out twelve men joined the Forces but temporary auxiliaries were found. In February, 1919, the chairman of the Fire Brigade Committee reported that during the war they had turned out for 108 official air-raid alarms and thirty-seven fire calls, "leaving their homes and families without demur immediately on receiving an alarm".

The brigade remained under the control of the council until 1940, when it was incorporated into the Auxiliary Fire Service. After the war the Essex Fire Service took over, and a new station was built in Fronks Road; the old one was converted by Essex County Council into an attractive residential hostel for courses in sailing.

As Harwich became a healthier and safer place to live in, the population rose and more accommodation was needed, not only for the

Above: *The horse-drawn steam fire engine belonging to the Great Eastern Railway fire brigade outside the fire station at Parkeston Quay. The photograph was taken in 1923, the year the GER was absorbed into the London and North Eastern Railway.*

Left: *The Harwich Fire Brigade's steam fire engine turns out about 1920. In the driving seat is young David Wills; standing next to him is the fire brigade captain, his father, also David Wills.*

Above: *The results of a fire at the tailor's shop of Mr Harry Read at 58 Church Street on 10th January, 1913. This was the first of a series of fires that destroyed other properties in Church Street; both the premises of the London Meat Company at 56 and of ironmonger Mr J. A. Saunders at 55 were destroyed in this way.*

living but for the dead. Churchyards were full. This was a national problem, and an Act of 1853 set up local Burial Boards to make the necessary provision out of the rates. Such a Board, consisting of six men, was elected at a vestry meeting in June, 1854, and bought land for a burial ground on Dovercourt Green. This land, it should be noted, the Home Office inspector recommended because of "the saving that would be effected owing to the same not requiring to be drained". Plans and specifications were invited from architects, with estimates for laying out the grounds, building a lodge and a receiving house or lych house, which could be used as an unconsecrated chapel by nonconformists; those submitted by Mr C. H. Edwards were accepted.

Things soon started to go wrong, and continued to do so, giving no grounds for believing that honest work was characteristic of the Victorian Age. The early experience of the Board may be summarized as follows:

May, 1855 Discrepancies suspected in Mr Edwards' quantities; an independent architect reported "gross inaccuracies" and poor work. Edwards dismissed and claimed £109 7s 9d due; Board offered £20; long arguments leading to High Court action in London ended when plaintiff offered to withdraw claim if Board also withdrew counter-claim; agreed when inquiries showed Edwards lacked the means to pay if he lost the case.

July, 1856 Horace Darken, new architect, reported "many defects and omissions on part of contractors" such as broken slates, doors and windows which could not be shut, unsatisfactory painting, glazing, plumbing and brickwork; long arguments with contractors.

August, 1856 Mr Butcher's tender to drain the cemetery for £60 accepted.

March, 1857 After many complaints, found that drains had not been carried to stipulated depth, so taken up and relaid to depth of ten feet.

August, 1857 Vicar reported everything in a bad state, and chickens being kept in the chapel. Sexton dismissed.

March, 1858 Drainage reported finished and satisfactory.

April, 1858 Water found in Mr George's vault and several brick graves.

May, 1858 Examination of contractor's claims showed the same items appeared several times, extras already covered in original contract.

March, 1860 Severe gale damaged gable ends, blew in windows, blew off slates, blew down fences.

July, 1863 New fence blown down again, posts found to be rotten.

July, 1865 "On opening Mrs Etherden's vault, 2 feet 4 inches of water was found therein"; a well, twelve feet deep, dug near the vault soon had three feet of water in it.

August, 1866 Reported cemetery much neglected and fowl wandering about. Sexton dismissed.

So it went on.

Educating the Young
7

THE CHURCHWARDENS' accounts for the parish of St Nicholas refer to a schoolmaster in the sixteenth century and a scholar from Harwich who entered Caius College, Cambridge, in 1581, but no details are given. Until 1870 no system of state education existed in Britain, and in Harwich, as in most towns, a few children received instruction in a charitable foundation, in private schools, or in denominational schools. In 1850 it was reckoned that forty per cent of the population was illiterate.

The Corporation or Free School was built by Sir Humphrey Parsons, MP, in 1724 on land given by the corporation in King's Quay Street "for instructing the youth of Harwich in good manners and the doctrine of the Church of England", and the vicar was paid £20 per annum to teach twenty poor boys nominated by the council. A report on the school in 1805 stated that he attended two or three times a week to inspect books, while "the principal part of the education of the boys is left to the usher, Mr Orms, who constantly attends". The "Plan of Education" and matters relating to hygiene and discipline were given as follows:

Monday	Morning; repeat Collects and read,
Tuesday	write, spell and cypher
Wednesday	
Thursday	Morning. Crossman's Catechism, Read and Spell words — with their meaning. Afternoon. Arithmetical Tables and Catechism
Friday	Morning. Read in the Prayer Book Afternoon. The same as Monday and Tuesday.
Saturday	Abbreviations, Church Catechism, Roman hand, and get Sunday Collects to repeat Monday morning.
School hours	From Nine in the morning until twelve. Afternoon from two to five.

The commitee recommend for a request to be made to Mr Whinfield that strict order, silence and regularity be kept, and, if any complaint is made by any of the parents for such strictness, to refer them to the Mayor.

Cleanliness	The Boys twice a week sweep the School, but the walls and every part appear very Dirty . . . Not any attention seem to be paid by the Parents to the cleanliness and dress of the Boys, most of them are in rags, and their skins dirty and filthy. The committee recommend that unless Children are sent clean, for them not to be allowed to go to the School.

There were then thirty-two boys, admitted at the age of eight and remaining at the school until they were fourteen. The headmaster, who lived in the house adjoining the school, was paid £30 per annum and had to provide books and stationery.

The children of affluent parents were educated at private schools or "academies". In February, 1769, Mrs Spratlin announced in the *Ipswich Journal* that she was opening a boarding school for young ladies at Harwich "where she intends teaching them all kinds of needlework, plainwork and lace, drawings of patterns, tambour, etc., also the English language, at 12 guineas per annum for board and education . . . day scholars 6/- a quarter. Writing etc. taught by proper masters".

An advertisement, also in the *Ipswich Journal*, appeared in 1760 for a rather unusual school:

At the Writing School in the West Street, Harwich.
Arithmetic in all its Branches, Geometry, Trigonometry and Algebra, with their application and Use in the Mensuration of Superficies and Solids; Navigation and several other branches of the Mathematicks; also the Italian Method of Bookkeeping, by Double Entry, are carefully and expeditiously taught by

WILLIAM ENEFER

He returns his sincere Thanks to all those Gentlemen, Ladies and others who have favoured him with the care of their children's Education; and begs leave to assure them that they may depend upon his utmost Endeavours to merit their constant approbation.
N.B. A careful, industrious, sober Person is engaged as Assistant.

During the nineteenth century the number of private schools fluctuated; a directory of 1848 lists seven, but Kelly's Directory of 1870 mentions only Miss Martha Taylor's ladies' school at No 8 Orwell Terrace and Mrs Marion Points' day school at No 60 King's Quay Street. Other unadvertised "dame schools" were to be found, such as the one described by an inspector in 1875. He reported that "after climbing a stair more like a chimney" he came upon an old dame living in one room, which "was made to answer the threefold purpose of a bedroom, a schoolroom and a kitchen, in which ventilation was a thing unknown".

Mainly as a result of the rise of Methodism and the awakening of the Anglican Church,

A group of pupils at the Upper Dovercourt National School shortly after it opened in 1868. On the right is the headmaster, Mr A. F. Goodey; his five children are among the pupils.

there was a growing feeling around 1800 that something should be done to improve the education and morals of the poor by building denominational schools, although many had misgivings about the dangers of giving the poor ideas above their station. The Church of England formed the National Society for the Education of the Poor in 1811, and in the following year a local committee was set up to raise funds for a National School. Fortunately, as the result of a dispute over the boundaries of Crown property in Harwich, some land reverted to the corporation and it decided to build a school on the site at an estimated cost of £450 10s for "the instruction of poor children according to the Reverend Dr Bell's system". This system enabled one teacher to teach an unlimited number of pupils in one room. The children were divided into groups, with each group under a monitor who was given information by the teacher to learn by heart. This was then imparted to the group in a question-and-answer fashion.

At first the school adjoining the church in King's Quay Street, which became known as the Esplanade School, was for boys, and a school for girls was built on the site where the old Fire Station now stands, but the boys' school was rebuilt and enlarged in 1859 to take both sexes, and the former girls' school became the first infants' school. The *Essex Standard* reported on 28th November, 1859, that the re-opening of the new school had been marked by

a concert of sacred music kindly given by Mr James Godball of Ipswich in aid of funds. The whole passed off brilliantly. An orchestra composed of thirty performers, played selections from Handel . . . The choruses were bold and thrilling, the flute and contra basso ably handled, and all performers gained the applause of a full audience who left highly gratified with the rich musical entertainment offered them.

The Corporation or Free School, erected in 1724, as it was in 1971 before restoration. Over the door towards the left is a tablet with the coat of arms of Sir Humphrey Parsons, the founder.

There were then eighty boys and forty-two girls on the roll, each paying twopence per week. The remaining income of the school came from endowments, subscriptions, an annual sermon, and a government grant that depended upon the size of the school, the average attendance, and the results of an annual inspection and examination in reading, writing and arithmetic. In 1871 there were 278 passes and 37 failures; the grant was £63 5s 4d and the headmaster's salary was not increased.

Results at the Corporation School were better. In 1875 all boys passed in all subjects; the grant was raised to £23 2s and the master's salary increased by £10 per annum, but it should be mentioned that only twenty-three boys were at school on the examination day instead of the usual thirty-eight.

White's Directory of 1848 mentions a school at the Wesleyan Chapel in Church Street, demolished in 1958 and now the site of Mayflower House, and the other chapels

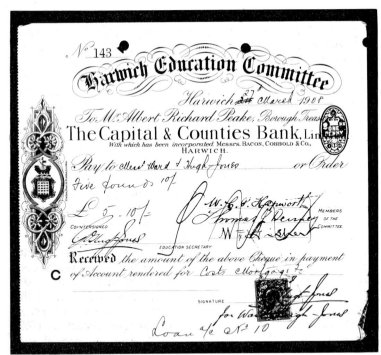

taught reading and writing at Sunday schools, though in Harwich there were no British Schools, as Nonconformist schools were called. As the town expanded westwards the Anglicans built a National School at Upper Dovercourt in 1868, and another in 1874 on High Street hill at Lower Dovercourt, while the St Nicholas's Mission Hall in Stour Road, Bathside, opened as a school for seventy-five boys and girls in 1879, and the Corporation School was enlarged to take 130 boys.

In 1881 it was reported that there was school accommodation for nine hundred children, and the Board of Education estimated that provision was needed for twelve hundred. The Education Act of 1870 stated that in such circumstances a local School Board, elected by ratepayers, might be set up to build non-denominational schools out of the rates, but in Harwich such a step was strongly resisted. The *Harwich Free Press* advised: "From a pecuniary point of view, it is of first importance that a School Board, with its expenses, should be kept at a distance", and the corporation tried

to do so by building in 1887 the Central School in Waddesdon Road to accommodate two hundred boys and infants. This did not fill the need, and five years later after the objections of the council had been stated at a public inquiry the Harwich School Board was set up.

New schools were planned, and when Mrs Jones announced in 1895 that she was closing her large private school, known as the Quay School, at the end of West Street, the Board took it over as a temporary measure. St George's School at Upper Dovercourt opened in 1894, the Avenue School at Lower Dovercourt in 1895, and Main Road and Bathside Schools the following year. At the same time the Catholic community built St Joseph's School, adjoining their new church on the triangular site later occupied by a filling station at the corner of Main Road and Station Road. As many had feared, the rates rose from fourpence in the pound in 1885 to 6s 3d in 1900 and eighteen shillings in 1920, but the Board was strongly condemned by an inspector in 1901 for "its unwise and pettyfogging parsimony". "Evidently", he wrote, "the Board regards willingness to accept a poor salary before character and qualification", and mentioned one case where a member of the Board justified a salary of one pound a week for a man coming into the borough by saying that "he ought to get board and lodging for 14/- or 15/- a week without washing".

When county councils were set up in 1888 they took over the responsibility for education beyond the elementary stage, and the Essex County Council financed local evening classes in French, German, cookery, dressmaking, shorthand, drawing, bookkeeping, woodwork and ambulance. The system of School Boards ended in 1902 when the education of children under fourteen was taken over by local Education Committees, and as there was no provision for secondary education in Harwich a new school was built on land belonging to Blue House Farm between Main Road and the Stour. The slopes on the northern boundary are known as the Hangings, and it was along

here that the railway line ran before Parkeston Quay came into being. The County High School opened in 1910 with forty boys and girls under the headship of James Valentine, MA. He was a strict disciplinarian, who by his insistence on the highest standards of effort and behaviour set the school on a road which brought distinction to many of its scholars. Until 1945 most pupils paid fees but some were awarded free places as the result of the eleven-plus entrance examination. As the number of pupils neared three hundred the Tower was taken over to accommodate a preparatory department and junior school, and remained in use until 1971, when it was relinquished after extensive additions to the main site.

In 1911 the Board of Education enforced the closure of Lower Dovercourt National School and the Corporation School because the accommodation was so poor, but work at the latter school had always been satisfactory, as the inspectors stated in their report in 1905: "The boys are very orderly and careful with their work, which is carried on under teaching of commendable diligence." The premises were taken over by the council to house the Engineer and Surveyor's department, and in return four scholarships were awarded annually at the new High School. The boys went to the Esplanade and the Central School. The former was on the Board's "black list" but remained in use until 1962, when it was demolished to make room for the Esplanade flats. The Central School closed after the Second World War and the premises were adapted for use as a County Library in 1947. There had been a strong feeling that a free library was unnecessary, and the offer of Andrew Carnegie, the American millionaire, to provide one in 1903 was rejected after a vote by the ratepayers.

Shortage of accommodation forced the Harwich Education Committee to build the Hill School for five hundred boys and girls up to the age of fourteen. It was officially opened in May, 1914.

After the Second World War a tripartite system of secondary education was established,

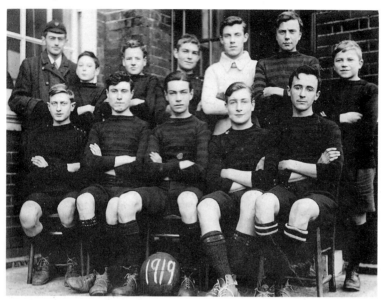

consisting of grammar, technical and secondary modern schools. The County High School became a free co-educational school for about twenty per cent of the total age group, selected after sitting the eleven-plus examination. They followed an academic course until the age of sixteen or eighteen, when many entered university or began professional training. Another group, amounting to about five per cent, was selected to attend the Gilberd Technical School at Colchester, and the Hill School became a secondary modern school for the remainder until the Sir Anthony Deane School opened in Hall Lane in 1957. The new school incorporated the lovely house and grounds called The Grange, formerly the home of the Misses Lilley, and provided a general education with more opportunity in practical

The Harwich County High School girls' hockey XI in 1928 smartly turned out in white blouses, dark-green gymslips and black woollen stockings, the normal school uniform of the period.

subjects for about nine hundred pupils. Boys could follow a course in navigation and seamanship and prepare for life at sea on the fully equipped ship's deck, bridge and masts which stood on the terrace outside the Navigation Room.

In 1971, three years after a large sum had been spent on new laboratories and other amenities, the High School was closed and all children at the age of eleven were sent to a comprehensive school for some fifteen hundred pupils, known as the Harwich School, on the site of the Sir Anthony Deane School. The former High School premises were used as an Adult Education Centre and enlarged to accommodate infants and juniors of the Mayflower School in 1988. This was the name given to the Hill School after 1957, and it was the decision to convert the buildings into a Magistrates' Court that brought about the transfer.

The Training Deck on which pupils of the Sir Anthony Deane County Secondary School were prepared for a life at sea. The school was officially opened by Rear Admiral Walter Evershed in March, 1958.

At the same time the Avenue School in Lower Dovercourt was closed.

Before the Second World War some well-to-do people sent their children to boarding schools such as Bishop's Stortford College and the Methodist school at Culford, near Bury, or to other local schools outside the state system. From 1909 to 1931 the Dominican Sisters ran a Convent School at Banksea House, at the end of Orwell Terrace, and in the nineteen-twenties and thirties Mr Haste had a day and boarding school called St Michael's College in Fronks Road. After the war it was converted into flats and the Red Cross Centre now stands in its playing fields. At the same time Mrs Shroff had a boarding school for juniors at No 1 and No 3 Cliff Road, where she awarded her assistants the Teacher's Certificate of Dovercourt College; while at 36 Cliff Road Miss Dunningham had a kindergarten where she devoted her life to instructing the young.

At the other end of the social scale were children who had the ability to win free places at the High School but were prevented by poverty from doing so. A scholarship paid the school fees, but there were no free meals or grants for school uniform and sports gear, and many families could not afford to keep children at school until the age of sixteen.

Sons of the Sea   8

IN VICTORIAN and Edwardian times many Harwich men, and a few stewardesses, spent their working lives at sea. Most of them worked on the passenger and cargo boats sailing from Parkeston; others served on fishing smacks, barges, lightships, tugs, ferries and other types of craft.

During the first half of the nineteenth century the chief maritime activity in the estuary was dredging for septaria, a stone found in the London clay which was broken up, burned in kilns and ground into powder to form Roman cement. The industry grew up after 1812 and proved a godsend to the town during the years of depression, but the long-term results were detrimental.

The Board of Ordnance, which owned Beacon Hill, began to take septaria from the cliff face and built a cement mill on the site now occupied by Angel Gate, where some two hundred thousand tons of cement were produced for government use before it was let. The right to take the cement stone from the cliffs at Dovercourt belonged to the lord of the manor, who leased it for a rental of between £500 and £600 per annum, but as the supply diminished this figure was reduced and in 1848 was about £300. In 1832 five factories were in operation in Harwich, giving employment to approximately 450 men, and although the number of firms had dropped to three by 1852, the same number continued to be employed. By 1859 John Pattrick was the sole manufacturer.

The removal of stone not only from Beacon Cliff but also from a wide ridge that had formed a natural breakwater caused erosion and brought protests from the council and landowners who suffered. These were ignored, and large quantities continued to be taken away at Harwich and at Cobbold's Point on the Felixstowe side. The consequences were very serious. As Beacon Cliff receded and the scouring effect of the tide was reduced the mouth of the harbour grew wider and began to silt up. After further representations by the corporation, in 1843 the Admiralty ordered Captain John Washington of HMS *Shearwater* to report on the matter. As a result the removal of stone within fifty feet of the foot of the cliff was prohibited, and a stone breakwater was to be built that would extend for eight hundred yards from Beacon Hill and direct the tide against Landguard Point. Work began in 1846, and four years later was stopped after £72,000 had been spent on dredging and £68,000 on the construction of 520 yards of breakwater. It was clear that more work was needed, and following an inquiry by a Select Committee of the House of Commons the preservation and improvement of the harbour was placed in the hands of the Harwich Harbour Conservancy Board, set up in 1863. The Board consisted of nine conservators: two were appointed by the Board of Trade, one each by the Admiralty, Trinity House, Harwich Corporation, Ipswich Corporation, the Ipswich Dock Commission and the Treasury, with another elected annually by the owners and occupiers of land in Mistley and

Left: *Cod smacks and a lightship moored in Harwich harbour about 1910. In the distance is the guardship HMS* Mersey.

Opposite page: *Two cod smacks lying alongside the quay. That on the left is a big ketch smack, and the smaller one on the right is dandy rigged, with only a very small mizzen.*

Below: *Beacon cliff seen from the harbour, as shown on Captain Washington's chart of 1842.*

Manningtree. The versatile Peter Bruff was appointed engineer to the Board, and Mr C. S. Tovell became the first harbour master in 1863, at £100 per annum plus twelve and a half per cent commission on all dues collected from shipping.

In *A Season at Harwich*, Lindsey described the "animated scene" on a summer evening in 1850 as several hundred smacks, each with a crew of three or four, raced for the harbour in order to be among the first to discharge the stone into barges at the Ordnance Jetty and Pattrick's Wharf. In the morning the race was on again for the most favourable positions for dredging at the West Rocks near Walton. Many of the boats came from Faversham,

Whitstable and other ports on the lower Thames, and the men had a reputation for toughness and hard drinking. Yet they were popular in the town, and when in March, 1845, a long spell of bad weather threatened to force some of them to enter the workhouse, £20 was raised locally for their relief, and the Harwich Temperance Association gave 266 loaves, with a message of hope that they would give up the drink.

By 1890 the cement industry was dead, owing to the introduction of Portland cement made from limestone. Pattrick made it for a time, using chalk brought by barges from the Medway, but was unable to compete with an area that had abundant chalk at hand and was

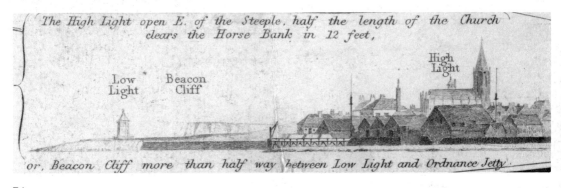

The High Light open E. of the Steeple, half the length of the Church clears the Horse Bank in 12 feet,

Low Light   Beacon Cliff   High Light

or, Beacon Cliff more than half way between Low Light and Ordnance Jetty.

near to the chief market, the London conurbation.

Efforts to revive the cod fishery in Harwich after the Napoleonic War were unsuccessful. In 1852 there were only five well-smacks, for the trade had gone to Barking, Gravesend and other places which already had the benefit of a railway and were close to the London market. It is likely that some Harwich owners followed the example of the Howards of Manningtree and accepted the advantageous terms offered by the Manchester, Sheffield and Lincolnshire Railway Company to move to Grimsby, where they could enjoy the free use of new docks opened in 1852 and free packing and rail transport to London.

Things improved after 1854 when the railway reached Harwich, and continued to do so until the 1880s, when competition from Grimsby and Hull began the decline that by 1914 brought the deep-sea fishery at Harwich to an end.

Much of the credit for the brief period of prosperity must go to the firm of J. T. Groom and Sons, founded by John Turner Groom (1794–1862), the son of a Suffolk farmer, who came as a youth to work at Harwich with his uncle Captain Hart, a lobster merchant. In

Alderman William Groom seen in 1882 wearing his mayoral robes. He was mayor eight times and was a leading figure in the cod fishery; he owned thirty-seven barges and built up a thriving business in timber, coal, cement, slate and other materials.

1838 he bought his first cod smack and soon added three more to build up a thriving business from fishing and importing lobsters from Norway. When he died the business was developed by his sons William, George and Samuel, largely on the initiative of William (1831–1910), the eldest son and senior partner, who was a remarkable man. He was mayor eight times, managed the Great Eastern Railway continental service from its inception in 1863 until 1867, owned thirty-seven sailing barges, founded a Penny Bank, and established a separate business as an importer of timber.

George Groom (1829–82) was mainly concerned with the organization of the fishery and

Cod chests in which the fish were kept alive until needed for market can be seen on the Camber in this photograph taken from the Continental Pier. A barge, newly launched from one of the Harwich shipyards, is moored alongside.

the management of the large office in Stavanger until his sudden death at sea. His brother Samuel (1839–1912) took over his responsibilities and was a respected figure in Stavanger and in Harwich, serving with his brother William on the Harwich Borough Council and holding the office of mayor three times.

About fifteen cod smacks of the fleet that worked out of Harwich came from Manningtree, Woodbridge and Aldeburgh. They sailed as one fleet and were ready to assist each other if necessary, but they worked independently. A similar number of smacks came from Harwich: the Groom family had fourteen at various times, Tom Denney, the principal local fish retailer, had three, while others like John Vaux, William Gane, John Watts, William Good and Alfred Middleton each had one or two. From September until Christmas they engaged in longshore fishing off the coast of East Anglia; after that they concentrated on the Dogger Bank, where they caught cod, haddock, soles and halibut until Easter,

making voyages lasting ten or fourteen days out of Grimsby. Some however worked all the year round on the Dogger and were away for up to eight weeks at a time.

From May to November they made voyages to Iceland, which could last six months, though they sometimes made two trips each season, each lasting about two months, depending on conditions. They made for the Orkneys and Faroes, where the deeper water necessitated the use of hand lines, about seventy-five yards long, to catch the cod. These were gutted, split, salted and stacked in the fish rooms until they were full; fish caught after then were put in the well. Some of the catch might be sold in the Faroes, but many smacks called at small Norwegian ports where merchants took the fish and supplied salt, coal, sugar, coffee, tobacco and other necessities. This might be repeated several times before they went a further 250 miles to Iceland to fill the fishrooms again with salt fish and the well with prime live cod. The average catch was about sixteen thousand cod, weighing forty tons.

From Harwich the salt fish and some of the "live" cod were sent off by rail to London. Before being sent to Billingsgate or sold in Denney's shops in Currents Lane and Dover-court High Street the fish were killed by "codbangers", who struck them on the nose with a club called a cod knocker.

Groom and Denney stored large quantities of fish in cod chests moored in Harwich harbour. These were like boats, eighteen feet long, made with slats to allow water to enter, each holding about a hundred and twenty cod in summer or eight hundred lobsters in winter. Groom's smack *Cobbold* lay at anchor with a permanent crew on board to look after twenty-four such chests, which surrounded them in tiers of four.

A smack could make a return trip to Norway in a week and bring back about twelve thousand lobsters in the well, spars of timber on the deck, and boards in the fishrooms for making coffins. Occasionally the well was pumped out to accommodate six Norwegian ponies. A smack had a crew of nine and several apprentices who served for about five years from the age of twelve or thirteen. Some of these boys were sent against their will by Poor Law authorities, and at Hull and Grimsby were brutally treated, but at Harwich, where they often had relatives or friends among the men, ill-treatment was uncommon, though boys were sometimes sent to prison for deserting the ship.

Mrs Groom took a motherly interest in the apprentices, who slept in the loft of the Groom residence when on shore and were well fed on suet puddings and gravy, followed by meat and vegetables. This was much better than the food at sea, where breakfast might consist of cods' heads, fish soup made from halibut fins and

Two North Sea fishermen in their seagoing gear of heavy duffle trousers and leather seaboots. Conditions at sea on the open deck of a sailing smack were anything but comfortable, and the men dressed accordingly.

biscuits, and dinner of salt meat, potatoes and "duff", which was described as a suet pudding without the suet. Biscuits as large as a man's palm and an inch thick were the substitute for bread, and were spread with treacle, broken up to put in soup or fried with fish after being soaked in sea-water.

On Groom's smacks an apprentice began as a cabin boy. One of his duties was to pour out the tea and say grace before dinner, a practice unknown on other smacks and a reflection of the firm's concern for the spiritual welfare of the men. The boys were paid £4 for their first year and an additional £1 for each successive year. The captain received about thirty shillings a week and the money from the sale of cod-liver oil, while the mate was paid twenty-five shillings a week, and the men twenty shillings plus a bonus of twopence a score for cod measuring more than the width of four planks when laid on deck, a plank being six inches wide.

By 1900 the system of apprenticeship had died out at Harwich, and owners began to sell their smacks or move to Grimsby, which had excellent facilities and enjoyed the advantage of being near to the fishing grounds and the densely populated areas of the north and Midlands. This brought an end to the Iceland voyages, but in 1900 there were still forty-two fishing boats registered at Harwich. Many of these were bawleys developed and built at Harwich by the Canns, Norman Brothers, and Vaux and McLearon. In the winter they were engaged in catching tons of whelks which the codmen used for bait, but early on summer mornings it was not unusual for a hundred bawleys to leave Harwich for the shrimping grounds that lay between Hamford Water and the Cork lightship. In the eighteen-eighties about half of that number belonged to Harwich.

They were said to have been called bawleys from the boiler used to boil the shrimps in sea-water on the return journey to Harwich. The shrimps were sold locally for 1½d a pint, but after regular merchants from Ipswich, Colchester and Clacton had been satisfied the bulk of the catch was sent in small sacks to London. This sometimes amounted to three

Left: Fred Good with a heavy catch of sprats about 1960.

Opposite page: Bert Good with his son Fred bringing in a catch of shrimps about 1935.

truck-loads nightly. In 1900 the Great Eastern Railway reported taking 955 tons of shrimps to London in one season. The large pink Harwich shrimps, the finest in England, were a great delicacy and much superior to the small, brown variety sold at Leigh.

Until the last quarter of the nineteenth century the trade in "sea coal" between the Tyne and Thames continued to flourish. The collier brigs and schooners were a familiar sight at Harwich, especially in bad weather, when with hundreds of other ships they took refuge in the harbour, but as competition from the railways brought a fall in freight charges so the owners were forced out of business, and by 1900 the colliers were seen no more. Since 1850 they had tended to concentrate on the London market while the needs of smaller, less accessible places were increasingly met by development of the Thames sailing barge. With its shallow draught and flat bottom, it could reach quays up the creeks and rivers of the Essex coast that were inaccessible to other seagoing craft; the crew consisted of only skipper and mate and possibly a boy; no ballast was needed, and by lowering the mast and gear they were able to pass under London bridges.

John Watts of Harwich, who had about ten barges, was the first to supply the local gasworks by sea and continued to do so until financial difficulties forced him to sell most of his barges in 1881. William Groom had a fleet of thirty-seven barges, and there were many other owners who traded mainly between the Orwell and the Thames, though they occasionally sailed to the Baltic and places up the Rhine. They were prepared to carry anything, the cargo usually consisting of coal, grain, malt, bricks, timber, cement, chalk, cattle food, bone meal, beer or fish manure; strangest of all were the "stackies", which could be described as floating haystacks. At remote places like Beaumont Quay, which belonged to Guy's Hospital, they loaded hay twelve feet high on deck, covered it with a tarpaulin, and lashed it down with the mast projecting from the middle of the stack. The mate perched on top to look out ahead and give instructions to the skipper at the helm. They took the hay to the Thames to feed the London horses, and

The wooden paddle tug Harwich, *owned by John Henry Vaux and built at Harwich in 1877, and the steam lifeboat* Duke of Northumberland *lying in the Pound in the eighteen-nineties. The* Harwich *was sometimes used to tow the sailing lifeboat* Springwell *to sea, but in 1881 she failed to reach the barque* Indian Chief *on the Longsand; Vaux was greatly criticised for the failure. The* Duke of Northumberland, *the first steam lifeboat built for the Royal National Lifeboat Institution, was stationed at Harwich between 1890 and 1892, and was then transferred to Holyhead so that the Institution could gain further experience of the operation of such boats; other steam lifeboats served at Harwich between 1894 and 1917.*

returned loaded with manure. Some farmers, like Mr Walter Wrinch of Erwarton, had their own stackies, and Ben Keeble, the master of his barge *Farmer's Boy*, set up a record by completing fifty-two round trips from Harwich to London in fifty-two weeks, during which time he spent fourteen days painting and refitting in the shipyard.

The first Harwich boat to be fitted with an auxiliary engine was a smack belonging to Bert Good, in 1919, and many barge owners followed his example in the nineteen-thirties;

Left: *An old-fashioned stackie barge at anchor, the stack of hay built up high above her deck and covered with a tarpaulin for protection. Such barges could load their cargoes at quays up the Orwell and Stour which larger vessels could not reach.*

Opposite page: *The spritsail barge* Gladys, *built by Canns in 1901, lies at anchor in the entrance to Gashouse Creek. She was a new barge when this photograph was taken; in the background is the Continental Pier with its goods shed, destroyed by fire in 1910.*

82

but by that time the only regular work available to them was to supply grain for Ipswich mills, and the trade was dying. In the nineteen-fifties Cranfield Brothers, who once had fourteen barges sailing, and R. and W. Paul Limited, who had twenty-five, began to sell them. The last went in 1967; motorized transport took over, and many barges, including twelve built by Canns, were converted into yachts and are still afloat. Others were bought to serve as houseboats or for charter work; some, such as the Harwich-built *Thalatta*, are now used for educational purposes while others lie rotting in the backwaters.

Life in a sailing ship was hard, and in bad weather a voyage in the German Ocean, as the North Sea was called, was particularly dangerous on account of the treacherous sandbanks guarding the approaches to the Thames. During the nineteenth century scores of ships and hundreds of men were lost each year on the Cork, Shipwash, Gunfleet, Sunk, Longsand, Kentish Knock and other sands, some of which were near enough to Harwich for local men to join in the work of rescue, salvage and pillage. The work was hazardous, and many scropers, as the salvagers were called, lost their lives, but fortunes could be made, and they

were prepared to take the risk. The law stated that salvaged goods must be handed over to the Receiver of Wreck, and that pillagers would be prosecuted.

From about 1800 voluntary associations raised money to provide rescue boats, and in 1824 the National Institution for the Preservation of Life from Shipwreck was formed to co-ordinate their efforts. Thirty years later this became the Royal National Lifeboat Institution, a move not welcomed by the scropers, whose livelihood was threatened.

Following the loss of several ships off Landguard Point in 1820, associations were formed to provide lifeboats for use off Harwich. The *Braybrook*, built in the Navy Yard by George Graham, was moored in the Pound, and the *Orwell*, built by Jabez Bayley at Ipswich, was stationed at Landguard Fort, but neither proved successful and they were soon taken out of service. The chief reason for their failure was that a tug was needed to tow them out to sea in a gale and bring them as near as possible to a wreck, but no steam tug was available. However the RNLI was assured by successive inspecting officers of Coastguard that no lifeboat was necessary, and such was the situation until 1875, when the nation was

The Norddeutscher Lloyd liner Deutschland *wrecked on the Kentish Knock in December, 1875, with salvaging smacks gathered around. On the right is the tug* Liverpool, *which rescued 173 survivors.*

shocked by news of the wreck of the liner *Deutschland* on the Kentish Knock with the loss of fifty-seven lives.

The *Deutschland*, which was carrying emigrants to America among her passengers, went aground in a snowstorm and her signals of distress could not be seen for many hours.

At that time Harwich had two steam tugs belonging to John Watts, seven times mayor of the town, and his son Walter, but when darkness fell and the rockets from the *Deutschland* were at last seen at Harwich, John Carrington, skipper of the tug *Liverpool*, decided that conditions were too bad for him to risk his ship before morning, when he took 173 survivors from the wreck. By then the *Deutschland* had been aground for thirty hours. When

the news of the wreck was reported in *The Times* there was a storm of protest at the apparent delay, for which Carrington was widely condemned, although the coroner's jury absolved him from blame. The Board of Trade inquiry into the disaster recommended that there should be telegraphic communication between lightships and the shore, and after Trinity House had spent eight years without success trying to achieve the same result using carrier pigeons housed and bred in the high lighthouse, the recommendation was implemented.

In 1876 the RNLI accepted the offer of £200 made by Miss Burmester, sister of the rector of Little Oakley, to provide a self-righting lifeboat, called *Springwell*, at Harwich.

Five years after the loss of the *Deutschland* J. H. Vaux, then mayor, was at the centre of another great storm of protest when the barque *Indian Chief* was lost on the Longsand. Vaux was on board his paddle-tug *Harwich* which towed the *Springwell* to within a few miles of the wreck before he decided, without consulting the lifeboat men, that the risk was too great. He returned, leaving the lifeboat with no other option but to follow him to Harwich. That night the Great Eastern Railway steamer towed out the *Springwell*, but the lifeboat, in the wake of that powerful packet, was almost dragged under the heavy seas; the crew, pounded by the great waves, was saved from certain drowning when the towrope eventually broke. The Clacton lifeboat also made a gallant effort, but Vaux refused to put to sea, and on the following day the Ramsgate lifeboat managed to save twelve of the crew, though

Alderman John Vaux in his mayoral robes in 1887. Shipbuilder and tugowner, Vaux took a leading part in local maritime affairs, but his action over the wreck of the Indian Chief *brought widespread condemnation. He died in 1894 at the age of fifty-two.*

seventeen had been lost. The *Harwich Free Press* echoed the general feeling in these words:

> A great weight of responsibility rests upon our present Mayor, the owner of the only tug in the port, who adopted such an extraordinary course. If it was not inhumanity, we should like to know by what other name it should be called. It makes one's blood run cold to think what must have been the feelings of the crew of the wreck when they saw a tug and the lifeboat approach them within two miles and then go away again.

In 1882 Miss Burmester presented another lifeboat, a second *Springwell*, which had ten oars as well as sails. It was too big to be housed in the shed which still stands near Timberfield, and had to be moored in the Pound. The RNLI rejected a fair offer by Vaux for the use of his tug so the boat was of little use until the first steam lifeboat *Duke of Northumberland* was sent to Harwich in 1890. It served as a tug until 1894, when it was replaced by the new steel, steam lifeboat *City of Glasgow*. These early steam lifeboats were not a success. There was scarcely room for the engine and boiler; firing was difficult and dangerous; the use of propellers or paddles was regarded as hazardous so they used a sort of jet propulsion, described as "sucking and blowing". The second *City of Glasgow*, which took over in 1901, had many improvements including a screw propeller, and remained in use until 1917 when the station closed down. When the second *Springwell* was scrapped in 1904 she was replaced by the *Ann Fawcett*, another sailing lifeboat, which stayed at Harwich until 1912.

The days of sail were numbered, and the Harwich salvagers, codmen and bargemen began to look for jobs with the GER or Trinity House, or perhaps did some fishing and shrimping. The steamships which replaced the old sailing ships were fewer but much larger, and though they were better equipped to avoid the terrible sandbanks they were more liable to suffer the fate of the liner *Elbe*, which sank after a collision off Harwich in 1895 with the loss of 334 lives.

The Harwich lifeboats in the Pound about 1912. The steam lifeboat is the second City of Glasgow, *on station from its building in 1901 until being taken over by the Royal Navy in 1917, and the sailing lifeboat is the* Ann Fawcett, *built by the Thames Iron Works in 1904 and transferred to Kingstown, County Dublin, in 1912. In the harbour is a light cruiser of the* Chatham *class; the bunkering of warships required as much as 10,000 tons of Welsh steam coal in 1908, and with the arrival of oil-firing an oil depot was established at Felixstowe.*

After 1918 there was no lifeboat at Harwich until the station was restored in 1967 with the *Margaret Graham* and an inshore rescue boat. Today the *John Fison* is a splendid sight as she lies in the Pound, equipped with powerful engines and wonderful navigational aids to remind us of the progress made since men could rely on nothing but their own physical strength to rescue survivors in the teeth of a gale. The work of rescue has been made easier but still remains dangerous, and Harwich may be proud that men are ready to volunteer to save lives at the risk of their own. Such men are not only serving in the lifeboat, for many heroic rescues have been made by local men working for Trinity House and the railway company.

Although an incalculable number of lives would have been lost without lighted buoys and lightships in the North Channel, Trinity House was surprisingly slow in providing them and usually did so only after repeated disasters had shown their necessity. Thus it was decided to station a lightship at the Newarp Sand and to build a lighthouse at Happisburgh after fifty ships and eighty fishing boats had been lost in a gale off the Norfolk coast on 30th October, 1789.

Trinity House had an establishment at Harwich in 1812 which became a depot serving eight lightships and two lighthouses, besides the new pair of lighthouses at Dovercourt which replaced those at Harwich in 1863. About a hundred men and their families were dependent on these lightships for a living, and the system under which they operated remained almost unchanged until the Second World War. The crew of a lightship consisted of eleven men: two masters, each serving for one month at sea followed by a month's leave ashore; three lamplighters, three fog-signal drivers and three seamen, who worked on

Right *Captain E. C. Mallows and some of the crew of the Cork lightship shortly before Captain Mallows' retirement in 1935. Models such as the one held by Captain Mallows were made by lightshipmen during their off-duty hours.*

Below: *The Trinity House tender* Argus *approaching one of the Harwich district lightvessels in the nineteen-thirties. A working party has been engaged on maintaining the lighship's cable.*

Left: *The high light of 1817 as it was at the beginning of this century. When originally built the light was half way up the tower at the same elevation as the earlier light, but this proved less than satisfactory and the lantern was moved to the upper floor of the tower.*

Below: *The 1817 low light with the "umbrella" shelter that was added in the course of the nineteenth century. As a result of changes in the navigation channel the two Harwich lights were replaced in 1863 by two screw pile lighthouses at Dovercourt, which if kept in line guided ships well clear of the tip of Landguard Point.*

board for two months followed by another calendar month at work on shore. They had seven days' leave a year plus bank holidays.

Once a month a steam tender, such as the Trinity House vessel *Satellite*, visited each lightship, taking the men who had been ashore to relieve those who had completed two calendar months at sea. A man brought with him enough food to last a month, and he also had a second month's supply for his mate on board. The man who was "off" looked after the interests of the men "on". In a large wooden box or a basket covered with canvas there would be fresh meat and bread to last the first week, after which they would fall back on salt beef and pork, tinned meat, flour and yeast to make bread, tinned milk, tea, sugar, dried peas, potatoes, onions and the large round biscuits made by Gould's or Cresswell's, which were often soaked and fried. "Sloppy hash", "dry hash", and onion pudding were common dishes, or, for a change, fish they had caught themselves or been given as a present by a friendly passing trawler.

When off duty the men played cards or followed hobbies of all kinds, making things which might be sold, such as rugs, mats, toys, models, ships in bottles, pictures in paint or sewn in wool, and slippers with rope soles and canvas uppers embroidered with a loved one's name. During the month "off" men worked daily from 8 am to 5 pm (1 pm on Saturdays) painting buoys, overhauling gear, and carrying out other maintenance work, and did seventy-two hours' sea duty, which usually meant three days on a lightship brought into the harbour for servicing.

Before the Second World War the routine was changed, and one month "on" was followed by two weeks "off". In the nineteen-seventies Trinity House began to introduce large, unmanned automatic buoys to replace lightships, and in 1989 the last manned lightship was removed from its station by the Harwich-based THV *Patricia* and brought into Harwich harbour to be laid up. The only remaining light vessels are unmanned, their equipment operated automatically.

The upper lighthouse of the pair erected by Trinity House at Dovercourt in 1863. The Dovercourt lights were discontinued in 1917; they have in recent years been rescued from decay by a restoration project launched by the High Steward, Mr William Bleakley.

Opposite page: *A large vessel on the Naval Yard slip, seen in a photograph taken by John Wiggins of Ipswich. She is thought to be the Dutch ship* Friesland, *which was towed into Harwich for repair in July, 1859, after she had grounded on the Longsand while on her way out to the Dutch East Indies with troops. The soldiers helped to haul her up using the capstan seen in the picture on page 13.*

Life Ashore 9

UNTIL the depression of the nineteen-twenties Harwich was a busy, lively place, and life ashore was vastly different from what it is now. In 1914 the Great Eastern Railway was the largest employer, after which came the Naval Yard at the northern end of the quay, leased from 1850 to 1894 to John Vaux and his son John Henry, who employed up to two hundred men.

Much of the timber needed for shipbuilding was imported by the Grooms from the Baltic and the Maritime Provinces of Canada; their massive black, wooden sheds and sawmill filled most of the quayside between the Great Eastern Hotel and George Street. Great logs of Oregon pine were discharged into the Pound, chained together and towed up to the timber pond near Dovercourt Station, to be stored in water until needed.

In 1914 Trinity House had no buildings on the quay; they were round the corner in George Street. Across the railway lines, at Gashouse Creek on Bathside, were the ship-building yards of J. and H. Cann and Norman Brothers, with Pennick's sail loft. Harwich-built barges were famous, and even men from the Thames admitted that Canns' were the best. Their last barge was built in 1914. William Blenkinsop McLearon, who was at the Navy Yard from 1896 to 1902, was succeeded by his son of the same name, who built his last barge in 1912 and went bankrupt in 1927.

The Harwich Barge Alliance, a mutual insurance club of owners, had 187 members in 1910. William Groom administered the funds from 41 Church Street.

The harbour was full of shipping, mostly wooden sailing barges, smacks, bawleys, brigs and schooners. Paddle-boats from Ipswich, tugs, continental and coastal steamers, and over fifty ships of the Royal Navy produced a pall of smoke which at times blew across the town.

From 1899 to 1909 HMS *Ganges* was moored in the harbour, and in 1912 the Admiralty made Harwich the chief base for two torpedo-boat flotillas operating in the North Sea. This was good for business, and Harwich was a lively place when sailors came ashore. The navy brought prosperity not only to the public houses but also to all kinds of other tradesmen, including the makers of the renowned ship's biscuits. In 1912 Sir Thomas Lipton, "the boating grocer" and owner of the yacht *Shamrock*, who had a shop in Market Street, opened an office and store on Halfpenny Pier and hired the mv *Pin Mill* to serve the fleet. Others, like Nalborough, the cheese merchant in George Street, followed his example. In 1859 C. H. F. Bernard, a naval tailor, founded a business which continued until 1979.

When men worked long hours and had little time for recreation Saturday was the highlight of the week. Plenty of shops in Market Street, Church Street and Currents Lane stayed open until 10 pm, selling off perishable goods cheaply to the crowds who thronged there. They came to meet friends, have a drink and

Left: *Shipbuilder John Cann with a half-model of a bawley, one of many built on the yard of J. & H. Cann. John was the shipwright, while Henry was responsible for the management of the business. The two had taken over the business when their father George was killed while unloading timber from a railway truck in 1889; he had built his first barge at the Bathside yard in 1877 after moving from Brightlingsea.*

Below: *Launching the barge* Kimberley *from Canns' yard in 1900. In the background is the gasworks.*

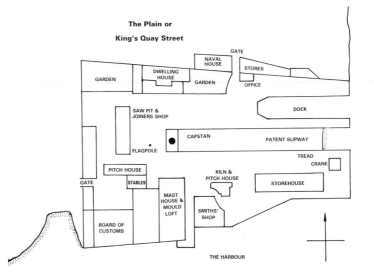

Right: *A plan of the Naval Yard as it was in the middle of the nineteenth century. The yard was first laid out in 1657, when the corporation agreed to lease the land on the northern tip of the peninsula, and it was enclosed by a ten-foot wooden fence.*

The Plain or

King's Quay Street

GATE

NAVAL HOUSE

STORES

OFFICE

GARDEN

DWELLING HOUSE

GARDEN

SAW PIT & JOINERS SHOP

DOCK

RIVER STOUR

CAPSTAN

PATENT SLIPWAY

FLAGPOLE

TREAD CRANE

PITCH HOUSE

KILN & PITCH HOUSE

GATE

STABLES

STOREHOUSE

MAST HOUSE & MOULD LOFT

SMITHS' SHOP

BOARD OF CUSTOMS

THE HARBOUR

buy fish and chips at Broomfield's in King's Head Street. There were not only sailors; men of the Royal Engineers and the Royal Garrison Artillery were stationed at the Redoubt, Angel Gate Battery and Beacon Hill Fort.

In the days before radio and television spending an evening at home was less appealing; the public houses were well patronized by men drinking and playing cards, dominoes or indoor quoits. Drunkenness was common among seafaring men, and the Salvation Army, Band of Hope, Good Templars and Rechabites fought hard to save them from the evils of drink.

Billiards was popular with all classes; tables were available in hotels and public houses, the Salvation Army Naval and Military Home, the Co-operative Hall, the Conservative Club at 32 Church Street, the Liberal Club near the Fountain, and the Constitutional Club in Church Lane.

Women and young people often found enjoyment in activities connected with church or chapel. There was also the Church Lads' Brigade, the Boys' Brigade, the Boy Scouts, Girl Guides and the Salvation Army Scouts. A building was used for a branch of the YMCA in 1870 but this project was short-lived. In 1904 a

branch opened at Seaview in Main Road, which had "a gymnasium consisting of dumb bells, Indian clubs, horizontal bars and other appliances", with instruction by "an old master of the gymnastic art, in the person of the Reverend E. Skilton". The YMCA did great work during the First World War, opening canteens on Harwich Quay and at Parkeston and erecting a large hut on the site now occupied by the Post Office and shops in Kingsway. With a concert hall, reading, writing and rest rooms, bar, and extensive kitchens to provide good meals, this was described as a home from home for servicemen.

Nice children at Dovercourt might stay with mamma quietly playing with their dolls and toys or reading, but the urchins in Harwich found their fun in the street or on the piece of hard ground enclosed by the sea wall beyond Gashouse Creek, known as the Bathside Mud. For a change they sometimes played in Canns' yard or Pennick's sail loft. Nearby was the *Anchor* quoits rink where they could watch members of the Stour Wanderers Club hurl steel quoits eighteen yards, trying to ring a pin set in a bed of soft clay. More exciting though was to see animals being killed in the four slaughterhouses which stood in the lane behind

93

Left: *The training ship HMS* Ganges, *built as a 2nd rate of 84 guns at Bombay dockyard in 1821, as she appeared when she was moored in Harwich harbour. She arrived from Falmouth in 1899.*

Left: *A naval seaplane flown to Shotley by Lieutenant C. R. Samson in 1912. Samson, who subsequently had an outstanding career with the Royal Naval Air Service, was seeking a site for a naval air station; it was eventually established at Felixstowe.*

Below: *The ships of the naval training establishment moored off Shotley pier in 1909. The nearest vessel is HMS* Ganges II, *built as the* Minotaur *in 1863, and inside her is the composite steam corvette HMS* Caroline, *renamed* Ganges *in 1908. To the right are a submarine depot ship and several submarines.*

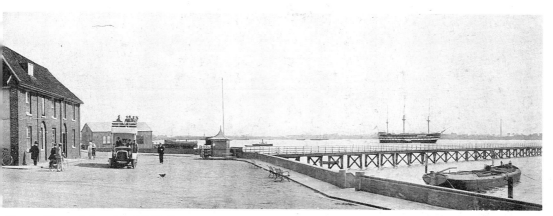

Above: *The training ship HMS* Ganges *seen from Shotley about 1905. Standing outside the Bristol Arms is the omnibus operated from Ipswich by the Great Eastern Railway.*

Right: *The mast-manning ceremony was a feature of life at HMS* Ganges *for many years. The figurehead of the original* Ganges *can be seen in front of the mast.*

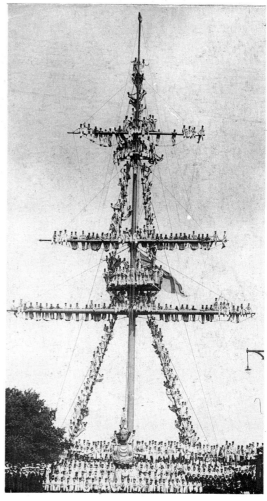

Ingestre Street and near the railway line. On occasions one of the beasts escaped and hell broke loose. There a boy could always get a pig's bladder if he wanted a ball to kick around.

From late June until the end of July schools were shut on Wednesday afternoons, deliberately coinciding with the shops' half-day closure, so that pupils might go on Sunday school treats. There were concert parties in the park, and at times entertainments in the street given by a German band, a dancing bear or an organ-grinder with a monkey. When the Electric Palace cinema opened in 1912 children could go in for a penny on Saturday afternoons. The Empire cinema opened in Kingsway in the following year. Before that time "magic lantern" and cinematograph shows were given in church halls and the Alexandra Hall. Plays were presented regularly at the Public Hall, built in Main Road in 1886 and converted into a Masonic Hall in 1907. In 1902 the management announced "a stupendous holiday attraction in the shape of Miss Winifred Maude's London Company in the world renowned musical drama, *The Stowaway*, which will be performed on Boxing Day and two following nights".

The annual fair and the circus were held on Bathside and the Barrack Field until 1912, when they moved to the Green. These, like the November "Guy" carnival and the regattas, were special occasions for all. Even more memorable events were the great national celebrations for Queen Victoria's Golden and Diamond Jubilees, the relief of Mafeking, and the coronations of King Edward VII and King George V.

From Whitsuntide onwards there was a succession of weekly camps on Barrack Field, mainly for regiments of volunteers who came to practise gunnery, but not before the Town Crier had gone round warning people to open their windows. The band of the Harwich

The staff of the Electric Palace in 1912. Included in the line-up are the two doormen, two cashiers, the projectionist and his two-and-a-half-year-old son, the manager and occasional violinist in his dress suit, and the pianist. The Electric Palace was built in eighteen weeks at a cost of £1,500 and opened on 29th November, 1911; it is one of the oldest surviving purpose-built cinemas in Britain. It survived two world wars and the 1953 North Sea floods, only to close suddenly in 1956 for economic reasons. In 1975 the Harwich Electric Palace Trust was formed to restore and reopen the cinema, which had by then fallen into considerable decay.

ADMISSION SIX PENCE

THE AMERICAN GIRL

THURS

Volunteers, formed in 1859, played regularly at civic and social functions such as the Royal Harwich Yacht Club regatta, when it played on the pier. The Salvation, Army band, founded in 1880, attracted a large crowd every Saturday and Sunday evening when it played on the quay or the Plain, and after 1911, gave concerts in the bandstand erected that year in Cliff Park.

Easter was celebrated in an unusual way. Good Friday was "skipping day", when the town turned out to join with sailor boys from Shotley and trippers from Ipswich in skipping with long ropes on the quay, promenade and the Green. It was a happy day, ending with singing and dancing in the streets, and probably a few bouts of fighting. The Harwich Regatta and Aquatic Sports were held on Easter Monday, not to be confused with the grand regatta of the Royal Harwich Yacht Club, held in Whit week.

When people who were born in Harwich before the First World War recall the "good old days" of their childhood, they tend to forget that for poor families living in dark yards, with a common tap and earth closet, life was hard. A labourer's wages were so low that it was hard to make ends meet at the best of times; when he grew old or was out of work

Above left: *The scene in Church Street on 22nd June, 1911, the coronation day of King George V and Queen Mary.*

Left: *Local people in their best clothes watch the arrival of the paddle steamer* Essex *on Whit Sunday about 1912. The Royal Harwich Yacht Club regatta would open next day, and the crowds hoped to catch a glimpse of royalty or of millionaires and their ladies up at Harwich for the regatta.*

The Church Lads' Brigade band from St Nicholas's Church seen on Bathside about 1912.

The newly-formed Harwich and Dovercourt Boy Scouts ready to take part in the coronation procession on 22nd June, 1911.

The Salvation Army Sunday school treat at Pound Farm. A banner in the background reads "Give us this day our daily bread", and cups of tea are much in evidence.

Left: *Mr J. D. Branch at the door of his boot and shoe repair shop in King's Head Street about 1920. All the premises seen here, including the Lifeboat Inn on the left, were demolished in the early nineteen-fifties.*

Opposite page: *William Went poses outside his shoe shop in Market Street about 1920. Not only did he give trading stamps, according to the notice in the window, but he also spoke French.*

Below: *When this photograph was taken about 1920 there were more than sixty shops in the parish of St Nicholas, and nineteen of them were in Market Street. On the extreme right, next to the International Stores, can be seen Mr Went's shoe shop, illustrated on the opposite page.*

through illness, bad weather or trade depression he depended on charity and the Poor Law. The late eighteen-nineties and early nineteen-hundreds were particularly bad. Funds were raised to provide clothing and boots to enable poor children to attend school. On Fridays Mrs Pattrick doled out free soup for children; at Christmas some were given a meal at the Naval Yard by Alderman W. B. McLearon, six times mayor, while others had dinner at the Public Hall and were given an orange and a penny.

Some better-paid workers joined friendly societies such as the Foresters, Buffaloes and Oddfellows. They spent convivial evenings together, paraded occasionally with their regalia and banners, and their subscriptions entitled them to assistance in time of need. These societies and trade unions administered the national scheme, begun in 1911, to insure low-paid workers against sickness and unemployment, but benefits were minimal. A poor widow considered herself fortunate if she could take in washing from ships or the richer folk in Dovercourt, although this meant ironing until midnight, and the children might earn a few pence by running errands, selling shrimps or hot rolls, fetching coke from the gasworks or disinfectant which the council gave away in George Street on Saturday mornings.

The Changing Scene   10

AS TRADE expanded at Parkeston so did Dovercourt, for most of the white-collar workers associated directly or indirectly with the shipping services made homes there. By 1914 Dovercourt High Street had become the main shopping centre, and many shopkeepers in Harwich opened branches. As those who could afford to do so began to move into more desirable residences the population of Harwich came to consist mainly of manual workers and their families.

Before the days of the motor car holiday-makers flocked to Dovercourt by rail and sea. At weekends the steamers from Ipswich were packed, and in summer there was a daily service between London and Yarmouth, calling at Southend, Clacton, Walton and Harwich. Some visitors stayed at hotels and guest-houses, while others found lodgings in roads near the sea; they spent most of their time on the beach, where they paddled, played games and joined in sand castle competitions.

In the eighteen-sixties sea bathing was allowed only from bathing machines near the Phoenix. These were covered waggons in which people changed and were drawn a short distance out to sea in order to enjoy a dip, far from public gaze. By 1912 bathing machines had gone out of fashion, and the landlord of the Phoenix put up twenty-one huts where bathers could change into "a sufficient dress or covering extending from the neck to the knee".

With the outbreak of war in 1914 the drift westward was halted, and Harwich shopkeepers enjoyed a short period of prosperity

when the harbour became the base for six cruisers, fifty destroyers, nearly a hundred minesweepers manned mainly by fishermen,

Left: *The jetty built in 1908 near the causeway to the low light at Dovercourt served as a landing stage for small boats. It was demolished in 1940.*

Below: *Visitors arriving at Halfpenny Pier aboard one of the Great Eastern Railway steamers at the beginning of the century. Goods supplied by local tradesmen await delivery to Shotley or to ships in the harbour; the baskets marked H.W.G. belong to H. W. Gould, a baker who was famous for his ship's biscuits.*

Above: *Looking eastwards from the Dovercourt lighthouse about 1906. A "bazaar" has been built at the corner of Beach Road to cater for the visitors.*

Right: *Bathing machines on Dovercourt beach at the turn of the century.*

Left: *During the First World War the Great Eastern Hotel served as a military hospital. Patients wore a drab blue uniform.*

Below: *A German target map of the Harwich area used to plan Zeppelin raids such as the one in August, 1915, which destroyed houses at Parkeston and made life unpleasant for members of the Harwich Force whose destroyers were moored in the Stour.*

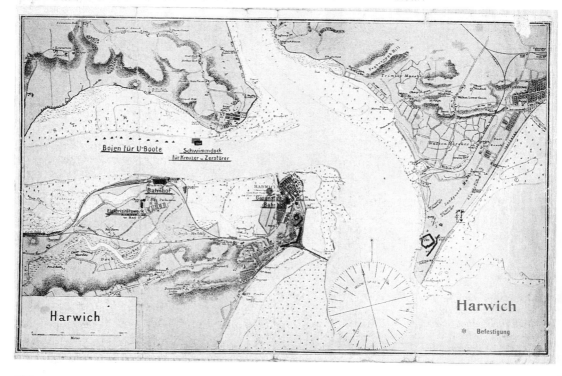

eighteen submarines with their depot ship, four seaplane carriers and a host of auxiliary ships. The Harwich Force of destroyers and light cruisers under Commodore Tyrwhitt (later Admiral of the Fleet Sir Reginald Tyrwhitt) saw a great deal of action in the North Sea.

The operations of the Harwich Force included some of the first air operations mounted from ships at sea. The vessels concerned were not aircraft carriers with flight decks but seaplane carriers converted from cross-channel steamers similar to those operating on the Harwich–Hook route.

The Great Eastern Railway steamers continued to sail between Harwich and neutral Holland, not without interference from U-boats and other German naval forces. The ss *Brussels*, commanded by Captain Charles Fryatt, twice eluded U-boats which ordered her to stop.

The *Brussels* was, however, captured in June, 1916, by a force of German torpedo boats and Captain Fryatt was summarily tried

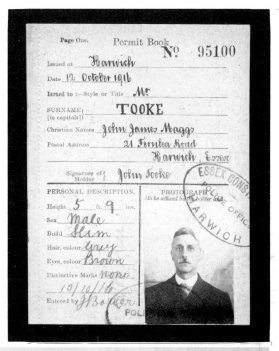

Above right: *An entry permit issued to a shipping agent's clerk authorizing him to enter the Harwich Special Military Area in 1916.*

Right: *Ships of the Harwich Force in the harbour during the First World War. An armed sentry stands guard at the entrance to Halfpenny Pier.*

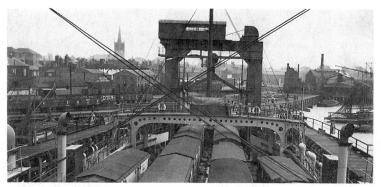

Left: *Harwich seen from the bridge of a train ferry lying at the train ferry terminal.*

Opposite page: *Prince George, later King George VI, opening the train ferry terminal on 24th April, 1924.*

Left: Train Ferry No 3 *leaving the terminal at Harwich for Zeebrugge in the early days of the service.*

Below: *A train ferry moored at the terminal is a prominent feature of this aerial view taken in 1935. A Trinity House tender and a steam pilot cutter lie alongside the old Continental Pier.*

by court martial on a charge that while not a member of the armed forces he attempted to destroy a U-boat by ramming; he was found guilty and executed at Bruges on 27th July, 1916. His death raised a storm of protest in this country, and after the war his body was reinterred in Upper Dovercourt churchyard.

When the war ended the Harwich Force was given the task of escorting surrendering German U-boats into Harwich harbour. Eventually more than a hundred submarines were moored in long lines in the River Stour, which became known to the local people as "U-boat Avenue".

With the return of peace many of the men who had manned the naval vessels operating from Harwich were demobilized, and Harwich stagnated. Victory was followed by dreadful years of depression.

In 1927, when the council opened a soup kitchen (a penny a pint) for the unemployed, the Navy Yard was demolished but the tread-mill crane was re-erected on The Green. The former Great Eastern Hotel stood empty, along with all the other industrial buildings on the waterfront. Grooms' did not re-open, and there was no shipbuilding on Bathside; however, a few fishing boats and bawleys were moored in Gashouse Creek, and the opening of the train ferry to Zeebrugge in 1924 did something to offset the disastrous fall in trade.

The three train ferries employed on the Zeebrugge service had been built during the First World War to carry wagons loaded with military supplies from the emergency port at Richborough in Kent to French ports, and were afterwards acquired by Great Eastern Train Ferries Limited for operation from Harwich. On the grouping of the railways they passed to the ownership of the London and

Left: *King's Quay Street from St Austin's Lane to the market was designated a slum clearance area in 1937. The buildings shown here were all demolished the following year.*

Below: *The east side of West Street from Church Lane to the Spreadeagle was also cleared in 1938. Nine years later Percy Hawkins erected a mock-Tudor fish shop and house on the site of the gabled houses seen here, and the town council filled another gap with a pair of houses.*

North Eastern Railway, but the special goods wagons they carried remained in the ownership of a separate company, the Société Anglo-Belge des Ferry-Boats.

The train ferry service ceased operations in 1988, but the 42-foot gantry which raised and lowered the link span giving access to the ferry remains as a reminder of a pioneering venture in which Harwich played an important role.

The government offered substantial grants towards work that would relieve unemployment, and the council took the opportunity to extend the promenade westward from Beach Road, build houses, and provide a swimming pool, boating lake and model yacht pond, putting greens and tennis courts. The first council houses were built on Dovercourt Green in 1920, and were followed by estates in Main Road, Parkeston Road and at Tollgate.

The houses in Harbour Crescent and on Tower Hill were built after the council bought the Green and all the land to Barrack Lane in 1930. Some of this War Department land was sold for private development, and when Mayflower Avenue and Beacon Hill Avenue were built the open land between Cox's Pond and Barrack Lane had disappeared. Many council houses were rented by families moved from

poor property which was declared unfit for habitation and soon lay derelict. Only a few shops remained open in Harwich, and when the Second World War came in 1939 the old town was dying, though Dovercourt was doing well.

The harbour again became a base for minesweepers, destroyers and submarines. The railway steamers with local crews were mainly used as troopships; these, with fishing boats, barges and small boats of all kinds, suffered heavy losses in the evacuation of the army from Dunkirk. When war ended, five passenger ships, two train ferries and many cargo boats of the London and North Eastern Railway had been lost, and many families mourned for sons and husbands. The war very soon had an effect on Harwich, for even before Dunkirk the town was having to deal with injured survivors from ships sunk by magnetic mines off the east coast. First there was the Dutch liner *Simon Bolivar*, bound for the West Indies with 383 passengers and crew, which was sunk not far from Harwich on 18th November, 1939, and only three days later there was the Japanese liner *Terukuni Maru*, which was blown up within sight of the shore.

Mines were even laid within Harwich

The market is prominent in this view of King's Quay Street looking towards the quay, taken in 1937. All these buildings disappeared soon afterwards.

111

An aerial view of Dovercourt in the nineteen-thirties, looking across to the River Stour. Pattrick's shaft, as the chimney of the old cement works was known locally, can be seen at top left; it was demolished on the outbreak of the Second World War.

harbour itself, and one of these sank the destroyer HMS *Gipsy*, broken in two by an explosion as she put to sea with two other destroyers, HMS *Boadicea* and the Polish vessel *Burza*. The latter was one of three Polish warships which escaped from the Baltic when Poland fell and was then based at Harwich.

When the Germans overran the Netherlands the destroyer HMS *Hereward* brought Queen Wilhelmina from the Hook of Holland to Harwich, and she travelled to London by train to form a new government in exile. Later Dutch warships joined the ships of the Royal Navy in Harwich, and a seaplane squadron of the Royal Netherlands Navy took up residence on the other side of the harbour at RAF Felixstowe.

During the five years of war Harwich was a front-line town, under attack from the air and with an enemy presence all too obvious if little seen out at sea. Air raids caused considerable damage to property in the town, though fortunately civilian casualties were few; only ten lives were lost.

On 3rd May, 1941, houses in Cliff Road were hit, and a fortnight later, in the early hours of 17th May, another raid flattened the old Ordnance Building, which had been taken over in 1931 by C. H. Bernard and Son, naval tailors. The then head of the firm, Tom

Left: *A fire officer and an air raid warden among the ruins of C. H. Bernard and Son's clothing factory after the raid of 17th May, 1941.*

Below: *Rescue workers pause for rest amid the wreckage of houses in Cliff Road, 3rd May, 1941.*

Right: *An ARP first aid party at Dovercourt soon after the outbreak of war.*

Bernard, was Civil Defence controller for the town.

"Bernards of Harwich" were known throughout the Royal Navy, both because of their work and because the name of the firm appeared on every "Housey" ticket—this game, now known as bingo, was the only gambling game officially permitted on HM ships. The firm had been founded as far back as 1895 by C. H. F. Bernard, who made the acquaintance of the future King Edward VII while serving as a ship's tailor and as a result made sailor suits for the royal children after setting up in business on his own account.

The old factory destroyed in 1941 was replaced by a new building, but the firm sold out in 1979.

After the war concrete defences were demolished and used to double the width of the promenade, while at Harwich the Great Eastern Hotel was converted into a Town Hall and municipal offices. The area bounded by St Austin's Lane, King's Quay Street, Market Street and King's Head Street, which government officials pronounced to be beyond redemption, was cleared and by 1955 had been rebuilt; after this it was decided to restore old property wherever possible, and with help from the government, Essex County Council and the Pilgrim Trust, the tide began to turn. The council had shown the way, and individuals took over the work of restoration. The Corporation School in King's Quay Street, which was almost in ruins, stands today as a fine example of work done by a former mayoress, Mrs Peter Holbrook. The quay took on its present appearance as Trinity House extended its activities and demolished old buildings to accommodate fine buoy yards, offices and pilots' headquarters. Both the piers and the boats which use them belong to Trinity House, bringing employment to hundreds. To complete the revival of the quay the old Naval Yard was swallowed up in a new Navyard Wharf, built on acres of reclaimed land and opened in 1962 for cargo ships trading mainly with Germany and the Baltic.

At Parkeston the story has been one of rapid expansion in car, passenger and freight traffic, necessitating the provision of a new terminal in 1972, but an event of momentous importance to the harbour and town was the decision of the

Regent's Yard in West Street was a product of the period when the gardens and orchards of fine old houses on the street front were being filled with ramshackle tenements to house the increasing population. In the photograph below, taken before the houses were restored in 1968, the arched entrance to Regent's Yard can be seen on the left. Further along West Street a man and a woman stand at the entrance to the adjoining yard.

116

government in 1984 to sell British Rail "Sea-link" ships and services to Sea Containers Limited. The new owners immediately began the first stage of the reclamation of the bay between Harwich and Parkeston, thus realizing a dream of over a century, and the provision of new berths, roads and services. At a cost of ten million pounds the Harwich Harbour Board dredged the channel to take ships of ten metres draught at all states of the tide. This opened the port to ninety-five per cent of the world's container shipping, and to the exciting prospect of its becoming a major deep-sea terminal. The shape of things to come was seen in the spring of 1986 when the *Koningin Beatrix*, a Dutch ferry-liner of 30,000 tons, entered service, but the announcement in 1987 that after sixty years the train ferries would cease to operate between Harwich and Zeebrugge was a painful reminder of changing trends in sea transport.

Probably as many people spend holidays in Dovercourt today as did before the war, but this is hard to believe because they cannot be seen. They now come to the caravan camp or the holiday camp and find amusement there. The band pavilion, which was once so popular, lost its appeal and was demolished as part of a scheme of coastal protection in 1972. Dovercourt promenade may be deserted, but during the summer and on a fine Sunday in winter the quay at Harwich is thronged with people content to enjoy the changing scene in the harbour or to wander through the narrow streets. It is often said that Harwich is a place which grows on you, and many have found this to be true. For them it holds a peculiar charm, which this book may help others to appreciate.

Harwich and Parkeston Football Club was founded in 1877 and first played on a field near the Phoenix Hotel and on Barrack Field. In 1899 the club moved to the present ground opposite the Royal Oak; at that time the ground was called Wix Meadow because it belonged to the vicar of Wix. The club reached the final of the FA Amateur Cup in 1899 but lost 1–0 to Stockton at Middlesbrough. In 1953 the "Shrimpers" again reached the final of the FA Amateur Cup, meeting Pegasus, a combined universities side, before a record crowd of over 100,000 at Wembley; Harwich and Parkeston were beaten 6–0.

Acknowledgements

ANY AUTHOR, if he is honest, depends to some extent on others who have preceded him. The present author acknowledges with thanks the help he has received from Hervey Benham's pioneering books *Last Stronghold of Sail, Once Upon a Tide, The Codbangers* and *The Salvagers,* and from Robert Malster's *Saved from the Sea,* all of which he strongly recommends to his readers.

He also thanks those who provided him with information, including Messrs B. Wood, H. Felgate, P. Howlett and H. Hitchman, and also Mr A. F. Waters for his help with photography. For their help in providing illustrations he thanks the Harwich Town Council, the Harwich Electric Palace Trust, Essex Record Office and Essex County Library, the Harwich Haven Authority, Mrs Winifred Cooper, Mrs Goodey, Mrs E. Lovett, Mrs N. Starling, Mrs P. Westlake, Captain R. Dove, Messrs H. Allen, Paul Amos, J. and R. Branch, G. Groom, Frank Hussey, R. Johnson, D. Morris and D. Rumble.

Finally, the author would like to thank Bob Malster, Terence Dalton's editor, whose knowledge of the maritime history of the east coast has been invaluable.

Bibliography

Dale, Samuel. *The History and Antiquities of Harwich and Dovercourt*. London, 1730.

Defoe, D. *Tour through the Eastern Counties*. East Anglian Magazine, 1949.

Hitchman, H. G., and Driver, P. *HMS Badger: Harwich, five years in the front line*. Published by the authors, 1985.

Hitchman, H. G., and Driver, P. *Harwich: A Nautical History*. Published by the authors.

Hitchman, H. G., and Driver, P. *Parkeston: A Century of Service*. Published by the authors, 1983.

Hughes, B. Carlyon. *The History of Harwich Harbour*. Harwich Harbour Conservancy Board, 1939.

Hussey, F. *The Royal Harwich: A short history of the Royal Harwich Yacht Club*. Boydell Press, 1972.

Hussey, F. *Suffolk Invasion: The Dutch attack on Landguard Fort, 1667*. Terence Dalton Limited, 1983.

Kent, P. *Fortifications of East Anglia*, chapter six, Harwich. Terence Dalton Limited, 1988.

Long, N. *Lights of East Anglia*, chapter six, Harwich. Terence Dalton Limited, 1983.

Lindsey, W. H. *A Season at Harwich*. London, Simpkin, Marshall; Harwich, J. Smith, 1851.

Malster, R. W. *Saved from the Sea: The story of life-saving services on the East Anglian coast*. Terence Dalton Limited, 1974.

Malster, R. W. *Wreck and Rescue on the Essex Coast*. Bradford Barton, 1968.

Moffat, H. *East Anglia's First Railways*. Terence Dalton Limited, 1987.

Patterson, A. T. *Tyrwhitt of the Harwich Force: The Life of Admiral of the Fleet Sir Reginald Tyrwhitt*. Macdonald, 1973.

Pollard, M. *North Sea Surge: The story of the East Coast Floods of 1953*. Terence Dalton Limited, 1978.

Strachan, C. *The Harwich Electric Palace*. Published by the author, 1979.

Trollope, C. "The defences of Harwich". *Fort*, 11 (1983).

Weaver, L. T. *The Harwich Story*. Published by the author, 1975.

Woodgate, J. *The Essex Police*. Terence Dalton Limited, 1985.

Woodman, R. *Keepers of the Sea: A history of the yachts and tenders of Trinity House*. Terence Dalton Limited, 1983.

Wren, W. *Ports of the Eastern Counties*, chapter eight, Harwich and Parkeston Quay. Terence Dalton Limited, 1976.

Index

Illustrations in **bold** *type*

A

Alden, John, 2
Alexandra Hotel, **45**
Alfred the Great, 1
Anson, Admiral Lord, **10**
Argus, revenue cutter, 12
Argus, Trinity House Vessel, **87**
Ark Royal, 1
Armada, Spanish, 1
Arrogant, HMS, **10**
Assembly Rooms, 14, 40
Avalon, paddle steamer, 24
Avis, Capt., 33

B

Bagshaw
  John, 38, **39**
  Robert J., 39, 40, **44**, **45**
Banks, 41, **58**, 66
Banksea House, **44**, **49**, 71
Barge Alliance, 91
Barges, 79-83, **82**, **92**
Barnard, John, 12
Barracks, 16, **17**
Bathing machines, **102**, 103, **105**
Baths, 14, **15**, **51**
Bathside, New Town, 50, **51**
Bathside Bay, reclamation, **20**, 117
Bawleys, 78, **92**, 109
Bayley, Jabez, 83
Bee, revenue cutter, 12
Berlin, ss, 31, **32**, **33**
Bernards of Harwich, 91, 112, **114**,
  115
Betts, Isaac, 3
Bigod, Roger, Earl of Norfolk, 1
Bleakley, W., **89**
Blue House Farm, 48, 69
Bowling green, 14
Boy Scouts, 93, **99**
Boys' Brigade, 93
Breakwater, 55, 73
Brickfields, 44, **45**, **49**, 55
Brookman's Farm, 55, 56
Bruff, Peter Schuyler, 20, 55, 56, 74
Burial Board, 63

C

Cann
  Alderman J. E., *frontispiece*
  J. & H., **51**, 83, **83**, 91, **92**
Carrington, John, 84

Cement, **8**, **46**, 73, 79
Cemetery, 65
Chapels and churches
  All Saints, 48
  Independent, 44, **51**
  Methodist, 46, **51**, 67
  Mission Hall, Kingsway, 40, **45**
  St Augustine's, 44
  St Nicholas's, 38, **51**
Charles II, 2, 3
Charter, 9
Chelmsford United Land Co., 40, 50
Cholera, 54
Church Lads' Brigade, 93, **99**
Cinemas, 61, 95, **97**
Circus, 96
Civil War, 2
Cleansing, street, 53
Cliff Hotel, 41, **49**
Cliff House, 38-40, **38**, **39**, **49**
  Park, 38
Clubs, friendly societies, 93, 101
Coal trade, 2, 10, 79
Cobbold, Thomas, 11, 14, 38, 44
Cockerill, Capt., 7
Cod fishery, 2, 11, **11**, **74**, 75-78, **75**,
  76, **77**
Concert parties, 95
Convent School, 71
Co-operative Society, 41, 49
Cork lightship, 83, **87**
Coronation, 1911, 96, **98**
Crane, treadwheel, **3**, **13**, **51**, 109
Cricket, 14, **14**

D

Dale, Capt. William, 31
Davies, Griffith, 7, 11
Deane
  Sir Anthony, 3
  Capt. Philip, 7
Defoe, Daniel, 9
Denney, Thomas, *frontispiece*, 76, 77
Deutschland, 84, **84**
DFDS, shipping company, 28, 35
Dispatch, packet boat, 5
Ditcham, Henry, 55
Dockyard, *see* Naval Yard
Dolphin, packet boat, 5
Doomsday Book, 1
Dovercourt New Town, **36**, 38, **41**,
  44, **49**
  development, 39-50, **49**

Dunkirk, 111
Dunkirkers, 2
Dunningham, Miss, 71
Dutch Wars, 2

E

Eagle, packet boat, 6
Education, 65-71
Edward III, 1
Edward VII, 96
Elbe, ss, 85
Electricity supply, 35, 57
Elizabeth I, 1
Erosion, coast, 45, 73
Esbjerg, 35
Essex, paddle steamer, **98**
Evangelical church, *see* Kingsway
  Mission Hall

F

Fair, 96
Fencibles, Sea, 16
Fire service, **51**, 60, **60**, **61**, **62**
Football, **71**, **117**
Foster Mfg Co., 30
Fountain, Harwich, 56, **56**
Fox, George, 5
Freshfield, Dr, 54
Fryatt, Capt. C. A., 107

G

Gane, William, 76
Ganges, HMS, 91, **94**, **95**
Garland, E. W., 30
Gas company, 56-57, **57**
Gas House Creek, **23**, **81**, 91, 93
Gasworks, 57, **109**
General Steam Navigation Company,
  7
George I, 5
George III, **10**, 17
George V, 96, **98**
Gipsy, HMS, 112
Girl Guides, 93
Good, F. & B., **78**, **79**, 82
Graham
  George, 7
  Joseph, 12
Gray, Thomas, 1
Great Eastern Hotel, 23, **25**, **51**, **106**,
  109, 115
Grimsby, 75, 77

Groom
George, 76
J. T., 75
Samuel, 76
William, 56, **75**, 76, 79, 91
Groom & Sons, 46, **51**, 75, 91, 109
Guildhall, **51**, **52**, 59
Gwynne, J. E. A., 41, 44, 46, 55

H
Hallsted, William, 14, **15**
Hamilton, Lord Claud, 25, **25**
Hankin
John, 1
Roger, 1
Harwich, paddle steamer, **81**, 84
Harwich Harbour Conservancy
Board, 73, 117
Harwich Improvement Act, 1851, 20
High House Farm, 50
High Street development, 41, **42-43**, 103
Hill House, 41, **49**
Hockey, **70**
Holly Lodge, 44, **49**
Hook of Holland, **30**, 112
Hordle, Rev. William, 44
Hospital, Isolation, 55
Howard's bath-house, **103**
Hunt, Capt. Maddison, 5

I
Iceland fishery, *see* cod fishery
Indian Chief, **81**, 84
Irresistible, HMS, 12

J
Jamestown, Virginia, 2
Jones, Christopher, 2
Jordan, E., 58

K
King George, packet boat, 7
King's House, **15**
Kingsway, 41, **45**, **49**
Kingsway Mission Hall, 40, **45**

L
Langley, Capt. Thomas, 5
Lee, Henry, 40
Lifeboats, **81**, 83-86, **86**, 98
Lighthouses, **72**, 86, **88**, **89**, **104**
Lighting, 53, 56, 57
Lightships, 86-89, **87**
Lindsey, W. H., 6, 19, 38, 74
Lipton, Sir Thomas, 91
Lobsters, 11, 75, 76, 77

M
Madre de Dios, 1
Mallows, Capt. E. C., **87**
Market, 9, **51**, **111**
Marlborough, packet boat, 5
Masonic Hall, 96
Mayflower, 2
Meteyard, H., **69**
McLearon, W. B., 91, 101
Middleton, A., 76
Mill House, 45, **49**
Mills, *see* Windmills
Model yacht pond, 111

N
Napoleon, 16, 37
Naval Yard, 3, **10**, 12, **13**, **22**, **90**, 91, **93**, 109
Navyard Wharf, 21, 115
Nelson, Lord Horatio, 16
Newport, Capt. Christopher, 1
Norman Bros, shipbuilders, 91

O
Ordnance Building, 14, **51**, 112
Orwell, ss, **19**
Orwell Terrace, 39, **42**, **49**
Oysters, 11

P
Packet boats, **4**, 5-7, **6**, 10
Parkes, C. H., 26
Parkeston
development, 27, 28, **29**
Quay, 26, **27**, **28**
Pattrick
J., 22, 45, 93
J. R., 46, **46**
Paving Commissioners, 53
Phillipson, Capt., 5
Phoenix Hotel, 103, 126
Piers
Continental (or Trinity), 26, **30**, **31**, **51**, **83**, **108**, 115
Corporation (or Halfpenny), **18**, 22, **51**, **104**, **107**, 115
Shotley, **95**
Pilgrim Fathers, 2
Police, **18**, 58-60, **59**
Poor relief, 37
Prince, packet boat, 5
Prince of Orange, packet boat, 7
Public Hall, 96
Public health, 53-56, 63

Q
Quakers, 5
Quays, Harwich, 20, 21, **51**
Quoits, 93

R
Railways
Eastern Counties, 19, 22
Eastern Union, 19, 22
Great Eastern, 23, 91
London and North Eastern, **62**, 111
British, 117
Railway stations, **21**, 22, 24, **49**, **51**
Ray Island, 26
Rebow, Sir Isaac, **72**
Red Cross Centre, 71
Redoubt, **8**, 14, 16, **22**, 93
Reform Act, 1832, 9, 38
Regattas, 96, 98, **98**
Resolution, 3
Revenge, 1
Robinson, John, MP, 17
Roche, Sophie, 6
Rochefoucauld, Duc de, 15
Royal Harwich Yacht Club, **51**, 98, **98**
Rupert, 3

S
St Michael's College, 71
Salvation Army, **64**, 93, 98, **99**
Salvation Army Home, **51**, 56, 93
Samson, Lt. C. R., **94**
Saunders, E. A., 30, 46
School Board, 68
Schools, 44, 48, 65-71, **67**, **71**, 115
Sea Containers Ltd, 117
Sealink, 117
Seaplane, **94**, 107
Sewers, 53-55
Shearwater, HMS, **12**
Shipyard, *see* Naval Yard
Shrimps, 78, **79**
Shroff, Mrs, 71
Skipping Day, 98
Slaughterhouses, 93
Sluys, battle of, 1
Smallpox, 55
Smith, G. W., 41, **43**, 48
Smuggling, 7, 11
Spa, Dovercourt, 39, **44**, **49**
Spinning, 10
Stevenson, Capt., 5
Submarines, **94**, 109
Sunday School treats, **64**, 95, **99**
Swimming pool, 111

T
Temperance, 74, 93
Thompson, Capt. Thomas, 2
Thornhill, Sir John, 5
Three Cups Hotel, 14, **51**, 61
Tilbury, 7
Timber trade, 91

Tollgate, 48
Tower, The, 46
Trafalgar Inn, 48
Train ferries, **108**, 109, **109**, 111, 117
Trinity House, 21, 41, **51**, 86-89, 91, 115
Turner, John, 11
Turnpike road, 15, 48
Typhoid fever, 54
Tyrwhitt, Sir Reginald, 107

U
Unemployment relief schemes, 58, 111
United Land Co., 50, 55

V
Valentine, James, 69, **69**

Vaux, J. & J. H., 76, **81**, 84, **85**, 91
Vicarage Farm, 50
Victoria, Queen, 96
Victoria Hotel, 40, **49**
Vine, The, 48
Virginia, 2
Volunteers, Harwich, 16, 96

W
Washington, Capt. John, **12**, 73
Watching, 53, 58, **58**, *see also* Police
Water supply, 53, 56
Watts & Son, 76, 79
Wembley, FA Amateur Cup, **117**
Went, W., **101**
Wesley, John, 6
White Hart Hotel, **51**, **54**
White Hart Lane, **54**

Wilhelmina, Queen, 112
William III, 5
Wills, David, **60**, **62**
Windmills, **17**, 45, **49**, **74**
Woodforde, Parson, 9
Workhouse, 10, 37
World War, First, 103-109
World War, Second, 111-115, **114**, **115**

Y
Yarmouth, ss, 33
YMCA, 93

Z
Zealous, paddle steamer, 24
Zeebrugge, *see* Train ferries
Zeppelins, **106**